INCENDIARISM

IN

GREATER NEW YORK

1912

IN NEW YORK CITY

BY JOSEPH JOHNSON, FIRE COMMISSIONER

1912

THE J. W. PRATT COMPANY, PRINTERS
52 TO 58 DUANE STREET, NEW YORK
77, '13, 6,000 (P)

Bare Rooms at 208 East 73d Street, Manhattan, Containing 12 Cents Worth of "Property," on which Members of the Fire Department Obtained $8,000 of Insurance. **(See page 43.)**

FIRE DEPARTMENT

PUBLIC DOCUMENT ON INCENDIARISM IN NEW YORK CITY.

Fire Department of The City of New York, Office of the Commissioner, December 31, 1912.

Hon. WILLIAM J. GAYNOR, *Mayor, City of New York:*

SIR—

I have the honor to transmit herewith a document on *Incendiarism* in Greater New York. For convenience in reading, I have presented the subject in popular book form, illustrated with numerous photographs, in the hope that the text will make a widespread appeal to the public, whose interests are so vitally affected.

The crime of arson is rampant in our city.

It is responsible for one-fourth of our fire-losses, involving an annual destruction of not less than $4,000,000 worth of property.

Despite all efforts of conscientious public officials, the strenuous activities of our Fire Marshals, and the detection and prosecution of numerous incendiaries, suspicious fires—particularly among certain well-defined trades—are on the increase.

Without exaggeration, our City is face to face with a grave public danger. It is essential that public attention should be aroused to the conditions which prevail.

The *Document on Incendiarism* here submitted does not stop at naming the evil:

It also suggests a remedy.

The document was prepared under my direction by Mr. William B. Northrop, a temporary inspector in the Bureau of Fire Prevention.

JOS. JOHNSON,

Fire Commissioner

Property Worth $3.44 on which Insurance Companies Issued $59,500 Worth of Insurance. On $3.96 Worth of Property they Issued $127,500 Insurance in the form of 135 Different Policies. (See pages 25-42.)

Twenty Cents Worth of Property in Bare Rooms at 220 East 36th Street, on which $19,000 Insurance was Obtained by Employees of the New York Fire Department. (See pages 40-41.)

FOREWORD

INCENDIARISM destroys each year $4,000,000 worth of New York property. This is more than $10,900 a day.

Nowhere else in the world is the "Fire bug" so active. In Europe Incendiarism does not exist, because Insurance Policies

Cannot be obtained without previous Inspection of Property and close inquiry into character of all applicants.

Everyone in America can get a Fire Insurance Policy for the mere asking. The New York Fire Department has obtained

No less than $127,500 worth of Fire Insurance, in the form of 135 different Policies on "property" worth only $3.96.

Dividing this amount, the following values were

Insured:					
Property	worth	$3.44	$59,500	in	Policies
"	"	.40c	59,000	"	"
"	"	.12c	8,000	"	"
"	"	.00c	1,000	"	"
"	"	$3.96	$127,500	"	"

A remarkable fact disclosed by the Fire Department Investigation is: Many Trades in New York profit by Incendiarism.

Rigid investigation into character of all applicants for Fire Insurance and previous Inspection of all property

Is the only way to stamp out the Fire-Making Industry. Fire Insurance Companies should

Stop the indiscriminate granting of Policies, and thus cut off the main motive for Arson. This is the only

Method of removing a SERIOUS PUBLIC DANGER.

CONTENTS

Chapter		Page
I.	INCENDIARISM IN GREATER NEW YORK	13
II.	INSURANCE AND INCENDIARISM	25
III.	INSURANCE AND INCENDIARISM (Continued)	34
IV.	TRADES WHICH THRIVE BY FIRES	43
V.	METHODS OF PUBLIC ADJUSTERS	50
VI.	"THE ARSON TRUST" AND OTHER CRIMES	56
VII.	CATCHING FIRE BUGS IN THE ACT	68
VIII.	SOME WOMEN FIRE BUGS	84
IX.	PROPOSED REMEDIES	100

APPENDIX "A"—German Fire Insurance "Proposal Forms"—Translated by Mr. *Robert H. Mainzer* ... 113

APPENDIX "B"—Replies of Foreign Fire Insurance Companies to Inquiries as to Methods of Doing Business ... 128

CHAPTER I.

Incendiaries Destroy More Than $4,000,000 Worth of Property in Greater New York Each Year; Causing One-Fourth of Total Fire Loss—Fire Insurance Methods Supply Crime Incentive—Organized Gangs of Professional Fire Bugs.

INCENDIARISM for the purpose of obtaining insurance money is estimated to cause the destruction of $4,000,000 worth of property each year in Greater New York. Besides involving the loss of this enormous amount of property, the crime of arson in this city is responsible for a number of deaths; and for endangering thousands of lives.

New York Fire Marshals estimate the fire-loss for the year ending December, 1911, at $12,470,806; but insurance authorities bring this total up to about $16,000,000; the difference in the estimates being due to the fact that insurance companies adjusted many losses which were not, until recently, reported to the Fire Department.

Accepting insurance figures as a basis of calculation, New York is being deliberately burned up at the rate of more than $10,900 a day. And this serious and growing loss is not due to accidental and unavoidable causes. It is caused by incendiaries.

INCENDIARISM A LUCRATIVE TRADE

The murderous trade of fire-making appears to be one of the most lucrative, and least risky, occupations pursued by certain classes of our population. Nor are these persons confined to what may be described as the criminal element. "Fire-making opportunists" are found in almost every grade of life; from the tenement dweller on the East Side, to the wholesale merchant in the downtown business district.

Among these people, a fire is looked upon as a blessing by no means in disguise. It is frequently the readiest way to realize a quick return on a slow-moving stock of over-insured goods; and is also, at times, the only available method of averting impending financial ruin. (See p. 47; also p. 60.)

Many fires, investigated by our Fire Marshals, are the direct result of financial conditions. An opportune fire bringing ready cash, appeals with peculiar force to a merchant embarrassed for funds, who considers that the most profitable method of disposing of obsolete stock is to "sell it to an insurance company."

Fire-making has become almost a fine art. So carefully are most of these fires planned, so ably are they executed, so complete is the destruction of all evidence of incendiarism, that detection and conviction of the crime are extremely difficult.

ESTIMATING THE PERCENTAGE OF ARSON

Definite data on which to base scientific estimates of exact percentages of incendiary fires is almost wholly lacking; and reports as to percentage totals for this class of fires vary among different authorities. Mr. F. H.

Ross, Metropolitan Branch Manager of three important Fire Insurance Companies, estimates incendiary fires as accounting for fully forty per cent. of the total number. The Fire Marshal of Brooklyn, Mr. Thomas P. Brophy, who has devoted much time and energy to the investigation of incendiarism, and who has many convictions of "fire bugs" to his credit, gives his opinion that arson causes 30% of the total fire-loss in this city; while the New York Fire Marshal, Mr. John P. Prial, an equally assiduous departmental head, places the figure at 25%.

Until additional facts, and tabulated statistics extending over a period of years, have been obtained, it is considered best to accept the estimate of 25% as a tentative figure which, if anything, errs on the side of conservatism.

A condition which permits the deliberate destruction of $4,000,000 worth of property a year, which imperils human life, and is such a danger to the community, well deserves close scrutiny at the hands, not only of municipal officials, who have the welfare of the city at heart, but of the general public whose interests are so vitally affected.

Others than the actual "fire-makers" are responsible for these conditions. And at the very forefront of the list are the insurance companies themselves. To borrow a phrase used by a president of one of the largest fire insurance concerns in the United States, the companies, by their lax methods, "place a premium upon arson."

INCENDIARISM DUE TO LAX INSURANCE METHODS

Mr. Louis S. Amonson, President of the People's National Insurance Company of Philadelphia—one of the best known insurance officials in the United States—speaks in no uncertain terms of crimes of incendiarism in relation to insurance; and, in a recent address before the Wisconsin Legislative Fire Insurance Commission, said:

> "If every fire is a crime against the State, it follows that every fire must be investigated by public officials before losses are paid; and, when this point is reached, our fire waste will cease to be a National scandal, for which insurance companies are responsible equally with the dishonest and careless portion of the people.
>
> "The company that fosters incendiarism by liberal payment of crooked losses and *the local agent who works hand and glove with the fire-bug by issuing policies without investigation are both a danger to the State; and, in the interest of public policy, should have their licenses revoked.* Every fire should be investigated by the State Fire Marshal, or the local police authorities, before the payment of the loss is permitted."

LEGISLATURE HOLDS INSURANCE COMPANIES RESPONSIBLE

In the findings of the Joint Committee of the Senate and Assembly of the State of New York, appointed to investigate corrupt practices in connection with legislation and affairs of insurance companies other than those doing life insurance business, the following recommendation was made in the Report dated February 1, 1911:

> *"When an application for a policy is received by an agent, he should take steps to satisfy himself that the risk is a desirable one."*

Failure to observe this condition is responsible for a large percentage of the suspicious fires which occur in Greater New York to-day. Were proper steps taken to ascertain the nature of risks, most crimes of arson and incendiarism would be automatically prevented.

IN ORDER TO PROVE THAT NO PREVIOUS INSPECTION WHATEVER IS MADE BY INSURANCE COMPANIES IN THE MATTER OF ISSUING POLICIES, THE FIRE DEPARTMENT, DURING THE COURSE OF THIS INVESTIGATION INTO INCENDIARISM IN GREATER NEW YORK, OBTAINED NO LESS THAN $127,500 WORTH OF INSURANCE IN THE FORM OF 135 DIFFERENT FIRE INSURANCE POLICIES, ON PROPERTY WORTH EXACTLY THREE DOLLARS AND NINETY-SIX CENTS ($3.96).

In issuing this large amount of insurance on this diminutive amount of property—consisting of a few trifling articles of household furniture—the companies made no effort whatever to ascertain the character of the risk they assumed, or the nature and amount of the property on which they issued insurance. (For full details of these transactions see Chapters II and III of this report, pages 25 to 42.)

EASE OF OBTAINING POLICIES MAKES INCENDIARIES

The facility with which insurance policies are granted at present offers a strong incentive to the commission of arson. Not only is it quite easy to secure fire insurance on worthless household effects; but unscrupulous agents—with the sole object of making commissions—assiduously canvass every tenement and small business house in the city, attempting to place as many policies as possible. Prospective insurers—many of them persons who, in their own country, probably never heard of an insurance policy—are urged to take out policies; the policy being regarded as a lottery ticket with the element of chance removed should the holder make his own fire.

Every claim paid by the companies is used as an advertisement to obtain more business. Owing to the enthusiastic work of agents in these districts, nearly every tenement dweller and foreigner in our midst has come into possession of a fire insurance policy; in most of these cases policies of $1,000 and more have been obtained on property scarcely worth as many cents.

That the interests of the public are affected by these conditions, not only directly—through danger to life and by loss of property—but indirectly through the payment of excessive insurance rates, is also obvious. Incendiarism is sufficiently extensive throughout Greater New York to cause high rates of insurance, not only in those localities in which suspicious fires most frequently occur, but throughout the entire city.

Insurance is recognized as a tax upon the population, and the raising of rates invariably acts as a hardship upon all honest persons who require insurance upon their property. As fire insurance is frequently the sole basis of credit in commercial transactions, this is a matter gravely affecting the business standing of the community at large. Insurance rates in certain localities are raised to an abnormal and arbitrary extent owing to the prevalence of incendiarism in these districts.

The attention of the Fire Department was first drawn to the making of fires as a business by an insurance broker in Manhattan, who made a statement to a Department Chief to the effect that he had been driven out of business in a certain section of the city owing to the prevalence of "suspicious" fires. His companies were refusing to issue policies in that section.

NEW YORK'S "FIRE-BUG" DISTRICT

In that particular neighborhood, bounded by the following streets: Madison avenue, between East 96th street and East 106th street, extending to the East River, more fires of a suspicious origin occur than in any other single territory in Manhattan. As a matter of fact, insurance companies have now come to the point either of refusing business from this district altogether or of charging very high rates to would-be clients.

From statistics in the Fire Marshal's office, it appears that in the one section alone bounded by the streets mentioned, there have been, during the last six months, beginning with January, 205 fires. During 1911, for the same period, there were 222 fires in this neighborhood; while in 1910, the number ran up to 243—this being a general average of more than 4% of all fires in Greater New York for the period mentioned.

Many insurance companies are still writing risks in the district, however, if not directly, at least through the larger brokers. Where an insurance company ostensibly declines a risk in this neighborhood directly to the person applying for it, little difficulty is experienced in obtaining the insurance when applied for through a broker, with whom the company wishes to remain on favorable terms. It is virtually an understood thing among companies and brokers that a certain amount of "bad business" will be permitted to the broker, provided he makes up for it with a proportion of business of a higher grade. (See testimony, p. 38.)

A CONTRAST IN NEW YORK FIRE AREAS

The map showing the fires and their percentages in this district will be found on the opposite page of this report. It is extremely significant, especially when taken in connection with the figures for a normal district, as set forth below::

In selecting a district of Greater New York to compare with that of the "fire bug zone," it was decided to use that section of the city lying within the following boundaries:

East 29th street to East 44th street, bounded between 3d avenue and East River. Here is found a mixed German-Irish population; while in the district compared with it farther uptown, in which so many fires occur, a population of more recently arrived foreigners predominates. It is true, the latter district has considerably more population, congested within a narrower area, than the former section; but, even so, there is an enormous discrepancy in the matter of fires. The occupancy in both areas is identical, flats, tenements, etc.

In the downtown section, bounded as above described, there occurred during January, 1910, but six fires; while in the uptown district, bounded between East 96th street and East 106th street, Madison avenue and East River, there were no less than 43 fires.

Taking the population of the "fire bug zone" as double that of the downtown section, there should not exist so wide a difference as that between six in the Irish-German section and 43 in the uptown district.

Month by month the figures work out similarly. We find that in February, 1910, there were only 14 fires in the downtown portion, whereas in the uptown district there were 27. In March, same year, there were 14 fires in what we might term the "normal" district; whereas in the "fire bug area" there were 55. In April of the same year, there were seven fires in the normal area, with 34 in the "fire bug district"; May, nine downtown, 50 uptown; June, five downtown, 34 uptown.

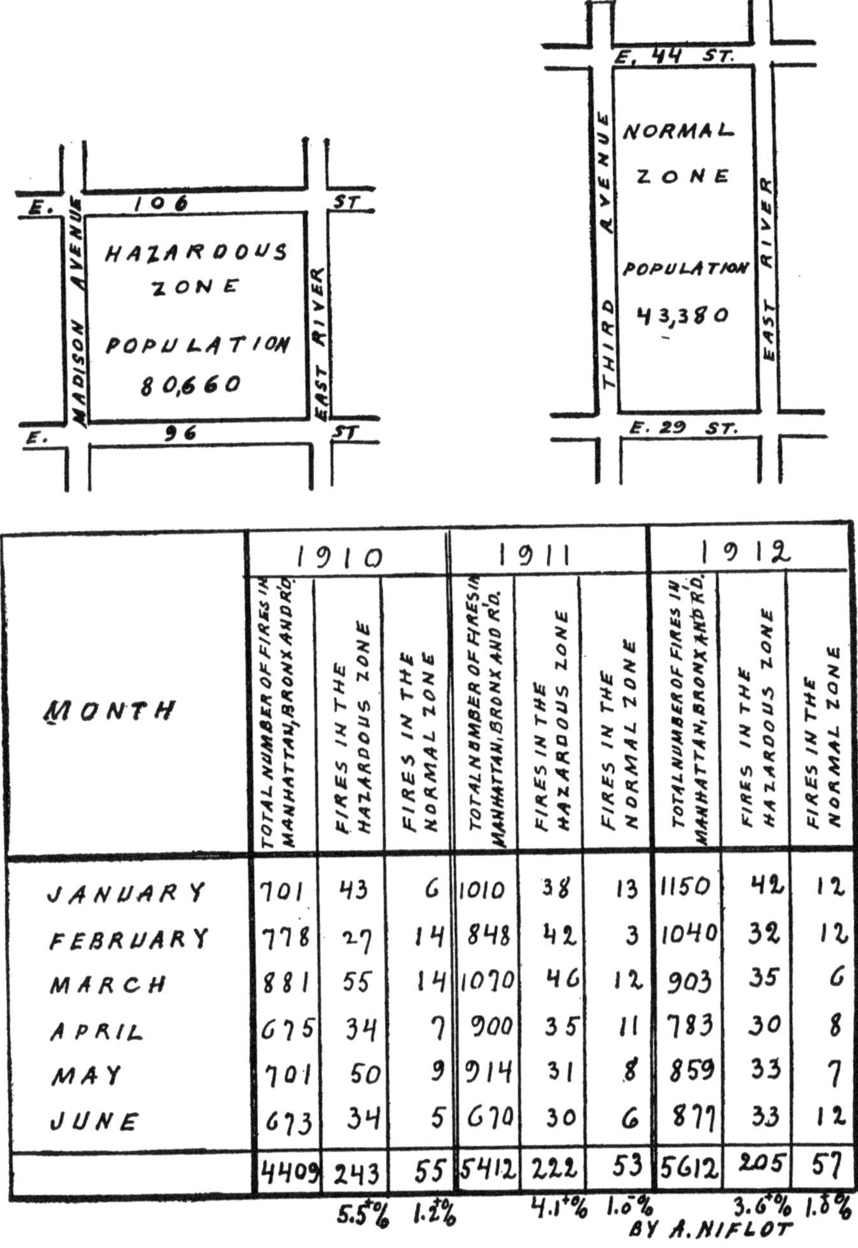

MONTH	1910			1911			1912		
	TOTAL NUMBER OF FIRES IN MANHATTAN, BRONX AND R'D.	FIRES IN THE HAZARDOUS ZONE	FIRES IN THE NORMAL ZONE	TOTAL NUMBER OF FIRES IN MANHATTAN, BRONX AND R'D.	FIRES IN THE HAZARDOUS ZONE	FIRES IN THE NORMAL ZONE	TOTAL NUMBER OF FIRES IN MANHATTAN, BRONX AND R'D.	FIRES IN THE HAZARDOUS ZONE	FIRES IN THE NORMAL ZONE
JANUARY	701	43	6	1010	38	13	1150	42	12
FEBRUARY	778	27	14	848	42	3	1040	32	12
MARCH	881	55	14	1070	46	12	903	35	6
APRIL	675	34	7	900	35	11	783	30	8
MAY	701	50	9	914	31	8	859	33	7
JUNE	673	34	5	670	30	6	877	33	12
	4409	243	55	5412	222	53	5612	205	57
		5.5+%	1.2+%		4.1+%	1.0-%		3.6+%	1.8-%

BY A. NIFLOT

Table Showing Number of Fires in East Side Hazardous Zone During First Six Months of 1910, 1911 and 1912, Compared with Fires in a Normal Area for Same Period. (For explanation, see pages 16 to 20, inclusive.)

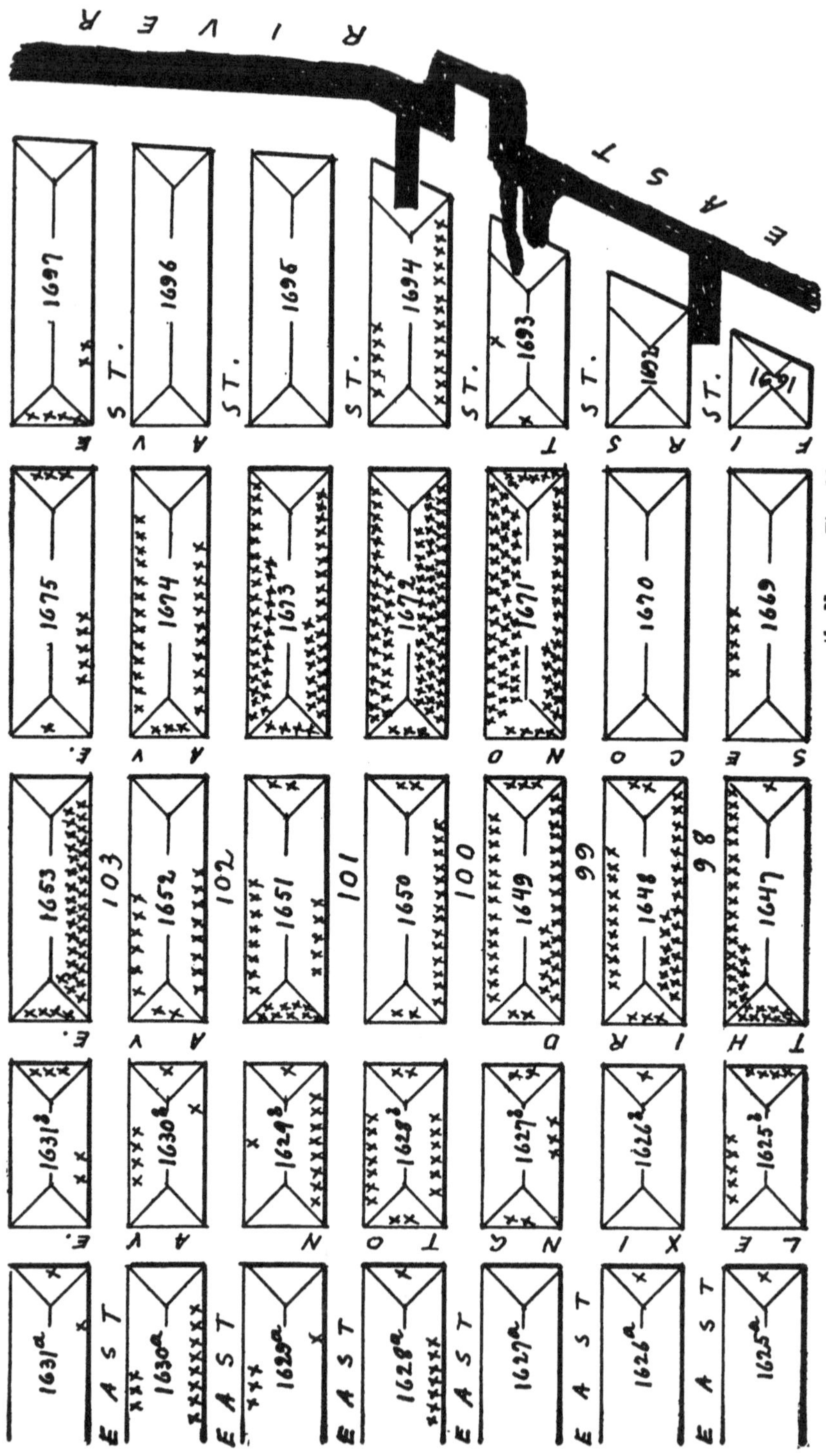

New York's Worst Fire District, "X" Showing Fires in Each Block for Last 2½ Years.
(For explanation, see pages 16 to 21, inclusive.)

Taking the year 1911, the same conditions prevail: January saw the normal district with 13 fires, with 38 for the contrasted district; February, three fires downtown area, 42 uptown; March, 12 downtown, 46 uptown; April, 11 downtown, 35 uptown; May, eight downtown, uptown 31; and June, six fires downtown, with 30 in the hazardous section.

PERCENTAGES OF FIRES IN CONTRASTED DISTRICTS

In 1910, the percentage of fires in what might be termed the normal section was only 1.2% of all fires for six months— the total number of fires for Manhattan and The Bronx, for six months in 1910, being 4,409; whereas in the abnormal, or "fire bug area," the percentage was 5.5%. Lumping the figures for 1910, there were, during six months of that year, only 55 fires in the normal section, against 243 in the uptown area mentioned.

During 1911, the total fires for six months in Manhattan, The Bronx and Richmond were 5,412, with a percentage of just 1 for the normal zone; while in the hazardous section, the percentage of fires was 4.1. Taking the fires for both sections, there were 53 for the normal area, with 222 for the fire-zone.

In the year 1912, taking the figures month by month, we had 12 fires in the normal area for January, as against 42 in the uptown section mentioned; February, 12 in the normal, 32 in the abnormal; March, 6 in the normal, 35 in the hazardous; April, 8 in the normal, 30 in the hazardous; May, 7 in the normal, 33 in the hazardous; and June, 12 in the normal, 33 in the hazardous.

Throughout the whole of the downtown district there were 57 fires during six months of 1912. This was 1% of the total fires for Manhattan, The Bronx and Richmond; whereas, in the hazardous district there were 205 fires for the six months; the percentage being 3.6.

The approximate population for the uptown section with an area of about 165 acres, is 80,664; while that for the normal, or downtown, district is only 43,380 with an area of 147 acres. But, none the less, the fires in the hazardous section are wholly disproportionate to those in the normal area, allowing for every consideration of density of population.

To sum the matter up in a table:

NUMBER OF FIRES IN AREA BOUNDED BETWEEN EAST 29TH STREET, EAST 44TH STREET, 3D AVENUE AND EAST RIVER —CONTRASTED WITH AREA BOUNDED BY EAST 96TH STREET, EAST 106TH STREET, MADISON AVENUE AND EAST RIVER

YEAR	Total No. of Fires in Man., Bronx & Richmond.	Dist. bet. E. 29th St. & E. 44th St., 3d Ave. & East River.	Per cent. of total.	Dist. bet. E. 96th St. & E. 106th St., Madison Ave. & East River.	Per cent. of total.
1910					
January	701	6		43	
February	778	14		27	
March	881	14		55	
April	675	7	1.2%	34	5.5%
May	701	9		50	
June	673	5		34	
		— 55		—243	
TOTAL	4,409 FOR SIX MONTHS.				

YEAR	Total No. of Fires in Man., Bronx & Richmond.	Dist. bet. E. 29th St. & E. 44th St., 3d Ave. & East River.	Per cent. of total.	Dist. bet. E. 96th St. & E. 106th St., Madison Ave. & East River.	Per cent. of total.
1911					
January.........	1,010	13		38	
February........	848	3		42	
March..........	1,070	12		46	
April............	900	11	1%	35	4.1%
May............	914	8		31	
June............	670	6		30	
		— 53		—222	
TOTAL.........	5,412 FOR SIX MONTHS.				
1912					
January.........	1,150	12		42	
February........	1,040	12		32	
March..........	903	6		35	
April............	783	8	1%	30	3.6%
May............	859	7		33	
June............	877	12		33	
		— 57		—205	
TOTAL.........	5,612 FOR SIX MONTHS.				

In this district, the operations of the fire-maker have worked an injustice to the whole neighborhood. Innocent persons, desirous of protecting their property by means of insurance, must, in this neighborhood, pay premiums many times higher than residents outside this abnormal area. In fact insurance rates throughout the city have been increased by incendiaries.

In the Legislative Joint Committee Report already referred to appears the statement that "*hazardous classes are paying less than they ought, at the expense of non-hazardous classes, which are paying more than they ought*"; and, in the section of Manhattan referred to as within the "fire bug zone" objected to by the insurance companies, we see an exemplification of this principle. Owing to the operations of "fire bugs" in this district, the entire neighborhood is virtually penalized by the insurance companies. All insured persons are paying high rates there simply because the companies accept premiums from *some* persons who should not be permitted to insure at all.

"FIRE BUG ZONE" DESERVES ITS TITLE

That the title "fire bug zone" is well deserved will be admitted when it is pointed out that a single block in this section, bounded by 100th and 101st Streets, between First and Second Avenues, has had, in the last two and one-half years, EIGHTY-FIVE FIRES. This is block 1672 on the insurance maps. It is somewhat difficult to obtain a policy there; though by applying to certain large brokers it may be accomplished.

On the south side of this single block the following fires have occurred during the period mentioned at the numbers given:

No. 301 East 100th Street 2 fires in the same house.
" 305 " " " 4 " " " " "
" 307 " " " 3 " " " " "
" 309 " " " 6 " " " " "

No. 311 East 100th Street	7	fires in the same house.
" 313 " " "	1	" " " " "
" 315 " " "	6	" " " " "
" 317 " " "	5	" " " " "
" 321 " " "	2	" " " " "
" 323 " " "	2	" " " " "
" 325 " " "	4	" " " " "
" 327 " " "	2	" " " " "
" 329 " " "	2	" " " " "
" 331 " " "	2	" " " " "
" 333 " " "	2	" " " " "
" 335 " " "	2	" " " " "
	52	

52 FIRES ON ONE SIDE OF A CITY BLOCK in 2½ YEARS. On the other sides of this same block there were **33 fires in** the same period of time.

ORGANIZED GANGS OF "FIRE BUGS"

Travelling between Chicago, Boston, Pittsburg, Philadelphia, Baltimore, Paterson and other cities, are organized bands of fire-makers who undertake "jobs" in any of these places. One of these gangs was, not long ago, operating in Paterson, New Jersey. That City, by the way, is almost a rival of Greater New York in the number of its suspicious fires.

Speaking of incendiarism in Paterson, Mr. John Stagg, recently retired Chief of the Paterson Fire Department, states that there is a regular club in that city composed of fire bugs, who will undertake to make fires at prices ranging anywhere from $25 to $60 and upwards. In his official report, dated July 26, 1911, he says, speaking of the abnormal increase of fires in his city:

> "The great increase is caused by the number of incendiaries and mysterious fires which were in the section of both sides of the river in the 1st, 2d, 4th and 6th wards. *A number of the insurance companies went off that section in stocks, in stores and furniture, but agents are again placing risks with the same parties which were refused before.* It is almost impossible to stop incendiaries unless we have the assistance of the insurance companies."

INCENDIARISM STOPPED BY INSURANCE RESTRICTION

It was amply proved in Paterson that insurance and incendiarism have a direct connection. Where companies declined to issue policies in certain districts, arson ceased. Where agents renewed their activities in those sections, crimes of incendiarism increased in direct ratio to the amount of insurance issued. Companies have again reverted to the old practices, however. There are incendiary districts in Paterson in which many suspicious fires occur; and yet insurance companies are still issuing policies in those sections.

The same conditions prevail in New York. The refusal of insurance companies to accept risks in districts where incendiaries are known to operate invariably acts in a salutary manner.

Insurance and incendiarism go hand in hand; and no radical change can be brought about in the conditions until insurance companies seriously grapple with the problem of previous inspection of all property on which application for insurance is made. Otherwise, incendiarism will continue, despite the

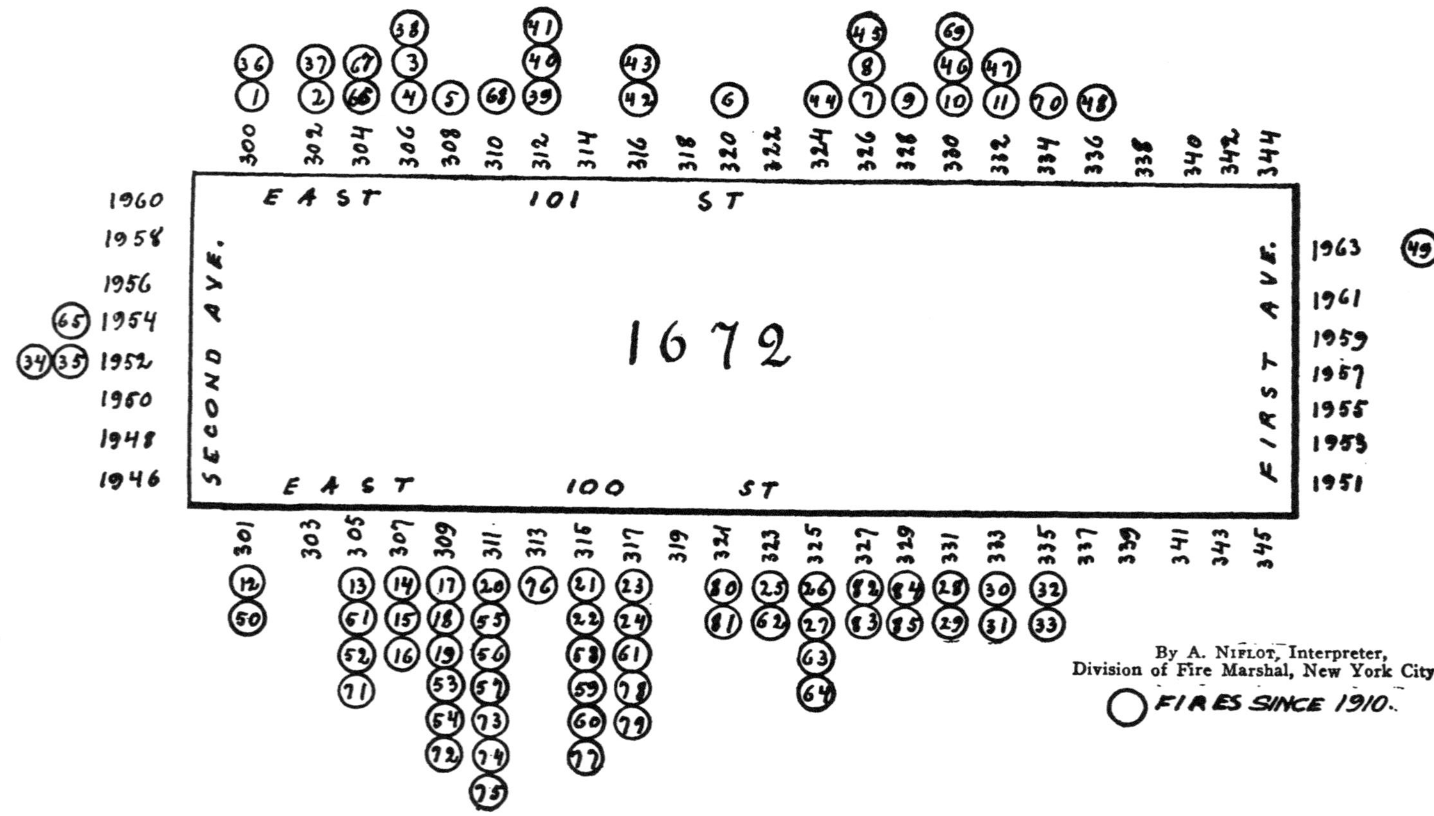

New York's "Fire Bug Block." 85 Fires in this One Block in 2½ Years.
(For explanation see pages 20 and 21.)

activities of public authorities to round up fire bugs. Convictions and prison sentences for arson are, after all, only "treating symptoms." No effective alteration can be made until the problem is dealt with fundamentally.

Insurance is one of the main roots of the arson tree. The cutting off of insurance policies will deprive this growth of its principal nourishment; and the elimination of the evil thereafter will present no insuperable difficulties.

CHAPTER II.

Testing the Question of Obtaining Fire Insurance Policies—Fire Department Agents Secure $127,500 of Insurance on Property not Worth $4—Extreme Laxity of Insurance Companies in Granting Policies Without Inspection—Names of Companies Granting Insurance.

IN order to test this matter of insurance, and to ascertain whether it were true that most of the reputable fire insurance companies of New York would grant policies to applicants without previous investigation, the Fire Department began in December, 1911, taking out insurance on household effects situated in various apartments rented from time to time in different parts of the city.

A four-room flat was first engaged on December 11, 1911, on the second floor of a tenement building at 239 East 101st street. The weekly rental was $5. This apartment, by the way, was in an exceptionally good location for observing the movements of certain persons whose occupation led officials of the Fire Department to suspect that they were connected with the "fire-making industry."

In order to "furnish" this apartment with the necessary "household effects" on which insurance policies might be issued, the following articles were purchased:

2 wooden kitchen chairs, at 81c. each	$1.62
1 small gas heating stove with tube	1.25
3 sash curtains, at 16c. each	.48
1 cuspidor	.09
Total value	$3.44

Upon the above-mentioned articles and including insurance at an address where there was no property at all, the Department obtained altogether the sum of $60,500 worth of insurance. On other articles of even less value, the Department obtained $67,000, making a total of $127,500 under 135 different policies.

The location of this apartment is in the midst of the "fire zone" interdicted by some insurance companies; and "rated up" by others. When officials of the Fire Department made application to insurance agents in the district, they experienced certain difficulties in obtaining insurance from some of the companies; though others were sufficiently acquiescent upon payment of the high rates demanded.

For instance, on February 15, 1912, Mr. Washington S. Howe, First-Grade Fireman detailed to the office of Fire Marshal, made application to an agent representing the National Ben Franklin Company in 125th Street, paying $2 for $500 worth of insurance upon the property named, at the address mentioned in East 101st street. Mr. Howe's connection with the Fire Department was unknown to the agent. Three days after making the application, the premium was returned to Mr. Howe by the agent, with the statement that the company was not taking risks in that section of Manhattan.

NEW YORK'S "BAD INSURANCE" DISTRICT.

This agent volunteered the statement that many companies refused to write business between 96th Street and 116th Street, east of Fifth Avenue. The rate charged, by the way, was just double the usual rate for fire insurance in other, or less hazardous, districts; the normal rate being $2 per $1,000 of insurance.

Shortly after meeting with this refusal, Mr. Howe succeeded in obtaining $1,000 worth of insurance on this property with the Caledonian Company, upon payment, however, of $6—three times the usual rate. The policy was issued through an uptown agent of the company, who remarked that the neighborhood was "objectionable" from the insurance point of view.

Various officials of the Fire Department then began a systematic application for insurance upon the $3.44 worth of property in the flat at 239 East 101st Street, and succeeded in obtaining $10,500 worth of insurance on these effects in this particular apartment. In no instance was their connection with the Fire Department known, either to the insurance agents or to the companies.

All policies but one were issued without any investigation or previous survey on the part of the companies, the latter seeming to satisfy themselves simply by charging an increased rate. In one instance, as high as $10 for $1,000 worth of insurance was asked, and a policy at that rate was issued by the Liverpool and London and Globe Company. This company, by the way, issued three separate policies on the property at this address, and in each instance charged a different rate. These three policies were as follows: No. 9473479, for $1,000, premium $10; policy No. 9275481, for $500 at the premium rate of $3; and policy No. 9274582 for $500 at the premium rate of $2. (See list of companies, page 31 of this report.)

ANOMALIES OF INSURANCE METHODS

As illustrating some of the anomalies of insurance methods, it might be mentioned that application for a policy for $500 in the Granite State Fire Insurance Company of Portsmouth, N. H., was declined on April 2, 1912, by the agents, T. Y. Brown & Co., on the address 239 East 101st Street, as will be seen by the following letter:

COPY

GLENS FALLS INSURANCE COMPANY
of
GLENS FALLS, N. Y.

T. Y. Brown & Co., Agents,
77 William St.

J. L. Cunningham, President,
R. A. Little, Vice-President,
E. W. West, Secretary,
C. J. De Long, Treasurer,
G. B. Greenslet, General Agent.

New York, N. Y., April 2, 1912.

WASHINGTON S. HOWE, Esq.,
239 East 101st Street,
New York City.

DEAR SIR:

Regret that we must decline line of $500 in the Granite State on your household furniture at above address, and thank you for the offer.

Yours very truly,
(Signed) T. Y. BROWN & CO.,
By LOUIS SCHAEFER.

POLICIES OBTAINED EVEN THOUGH FIRST REFUSED

However, despite this refusal, on May 14, 1912, a *policy in the Granite State was issued for* $500 *on the same address which had been declined on April* 2, 1912. The policy—No. 851460—was issued through Messrs. Benedict & Benedict, who seemed to experience no difficulty in placing the insurance, even in the " fire-bug zone," at very little above the ordinary rate. This instance may possibly have some bearing on the allegation that companies will often accept from certain agents or brokers doing a large business, risks in questionable districts; which, ordinarily, they would decline.

It is alleged that large brokers and agents are allowed to " put over " a considerable amount of risky business, provided they will generously interlard it with good accounts. The possibility of encouraging incendiaries does not seem to have presented itself to the companies indulging in this practice. (See testimony, p. 38.)

Another company which declined the risk at 239 East 101st street was the German Alliance Insurance Company of New York, through their agent, Michael Wohn, 1195 Washington Avenue, New York City. His letter is given below:

COPY
(fire)
GERMAN ALLIANCE INSURANCE COMPANY,
NEW YORK.

Branch Office: 1195 Washington Avenue,
New York City.
Michael Wohn, Manager.

New York, April 6, 1912.

MR. WASHINGTON A. HOWE,
239 East 101st Street,
New York City.

DEAR SIR:

Referring to your application for $500.00 insurance to cover your household furniture at 239 East 101st Street, I am very sorry to advise that we cannot take this insurance. I trust you will have no difficulty placing this elsewhere.

Yours very truly,
(Signed) MICHAEL WOHN.

As will be seen by the letter next offered, Messrs. Herbertz & Miller, 406 East 149th Street, also declined to issue a policy on 239 East 101st Street. These agents are branch managers of the following companies, as will be seen from their letter-headings: Germania Fire Insurance Company, North British & Mercantile Insurance Company, Sun Fire Office of London, North River Insurance Company, Aachen & Munich Insurance Company, Casualty Company of America, and Peoples Surety Company.

COPY

Fred. W. Herbertz   Philip Miller

HERBERTZ & MILLER,
Insurance Agency.
REALTY BUILDING.
406 East 149th Street, Corner Third Avenue.

Branch Managers:
Germania Fire Ins. Co.
N. British & Mercantile
Insurance Co.
Sun Fire Office of London.
North River Insurance Co.
Aachen & Munich Insurance Co.
Casualty Company of America.
Peoples Surety Company.

New York, April 9, 1912.

Mr. WASHINGTON S. HOWE,
239 East 101st Street,
New York City.

DEAR SIR:

Regret very much, but must decline your application for $500 insurance on household furniture, at the above address.

Thanking you, however, for the offer, we beg to remain,

Yours truly,
(Signed) HERBERTZ & MILLER.

Inspection of list of companies issuing policies at this address in East 101st Street, page 31 of this report, shows that *both the Sun Fire Insurance Company and the Germania had previously issued policies,* the Sun policy being numbered 8513024, and that of the Germania numbered 616941.

AGENT INSPECTS " PROPERTY " AND ISSUES POLICY

In reference to the granting of the policy in the Germania Fire Insurance Company, a curious incident occurred: One of the employees of the company at the Uptown Branch office in 25th Street stated that he would like to look over the premises before issuing the policy. He came up to the flat, looked over the scanty " household effects "—two chairs and a diminutive gas heater—in an otherwise bare apartment. After inspecting the place the agent suggested:

" Perhaps you have not moved in all your stuff yet?"

First-grade Fireman Howe, not wishing to make any statement that would be misleading, replied to this inquiry by saying that the policy was not wanted " just then."

However, in a few days, Mr. Howe called at a branch office of the Germania Insurance Company and the policy for $500 was handed to him, upon payment of $2.50. Here was a case in which an actual inspection of the premises was made by a representative of one of the largest companies, and yet the policy was granted, even though all indications pointed to the " risk " being an undesirable one.

Another company charging a high premium on this apartment was the Northwestern National of Milwaukee, which asked $4 for $1,000 of insurance, and issued the policy with no investigation. The Williamsburgh City Fire Insurance Company of Brooklyn charged a premium of $3 for $500 worth of insurance, while the Germania Fire Insurance Company of New York charged $2.50 for $500.

Altogether, *sixteen of the largest companies of New York issued no less than* $10,500 *worth of insurance on the scanty furniture worth* $3.44, *which stood in the bare rooms at* 239 *East* 101*st Street.* With but one exception, no investigation or inspection was made, and the company whose agent actually made the inspection, issued the policy just the same. Furthermore, *one of the largest companies—The Liverpool and London and Globe—issued three policies on the same property* at this address without anyone in the office of the company asking any questions or suspecting any irregularity, owing to applications having been filed for previous policies on identically the same property.

Had a gang of " fire bugs " been planning a haul, they would have been able to procure $10,500 worth of policies from these companies.

WITH SUCH A LARGE SUM OF INSURANCE ISSUED UPON LESS THAN $4 WORTH OF EFFECTS, IS IT ANY WONDER THAT INCENDIARISM IS RIFE IN OUR CITY?

It might be well in this place, even at the risk of repetition, to quote again the remark of Mr. Amonson, on the question of the issuance of policies by insurance companies without previous investigation:

> " The company that fosters incendiarism by liberal payment of crooked losses, and the local agent who works hand and glove with the fire-bug, *by issuing the policies without investigation,* are both a danger to the State; and, in the interests of public policy should have their licenses revoked."

The following letter from Mr. F. H. Ross will throw additional light on the overpayment of losses by insurance companies:

COPY

JOSEPH JOHNSON, Jr., Esq.,
Fire Commissioner,
157 East 67th Street,
New York, N. Y.

DEAR MR. COMMISSIONER:

A great *many arson fires in this city are caused by certain insurance companies in this town,* who deliberately conduct their loss paying department in the following manner, namely:

They advertise their business by *deliberately overpaying losses.* This may seem strange to come from me, but it is a fact, and it is well known who these companies are. A man makes a claim for $250 and they know very well his loss is only $150, but they will pay him $250 *if the broker in the case will promise them some business.*

That is another cause of a great many crooked fires and I do not know how you are going to prevent this.

Very truly yours,
(signed) F. H. Ross.

BY SYSTEMATICALLY APPLYING TO THE OFFICES OF THE VARIOUS COMPANIES OR THEIR AGENTS, THE FIRE DEPARTMENT HAS BEEN ABLE TO SECURE, AS STATED, THE SUM OF $127,500 WORTH OF INSURANCE AT VARIOUS ADDRESSES IN THE FORM OF 135 DIFFERENT POLICIES, AND NOW HOLDS THE SAME.

Nor was the procuring of this insurance a matter of difficulty on the part of those making the applications.

Fire insurance companies operate through agents or brokers, and the principal agents and brokers act through minor agents, from whom they are usually willing to accept business without question.

When an outside applicant desires insurance " direct "—that is, without having the application pass through an agency—it usually attracts some comment; seldom sufficient, however, as will appear from a perusal of the portion of this report describing how the insurance was obtained, to justify refusal on the part of the company; especially where payment accompanies the application.

Quite a large number of policies on the meagre effects mentioned were obtained without any payment whatever on the part of applicants. In fact, out of a total of $127,500 worth of insurance for which actual policies were issued, nearly two-thirds, or $79,500 worth, were granted by the companies or their agents without any payment whatever.

Persons applying for insurance are often allowed 45 days or longer before payment is actually demanded. This is done in accordance with the following regulation, which, in some cases, is printed on the forms issued by the agents:

> " New York Fire Insurance Exchange, Section 20, PAYMENT "OF PREMIUMS: All premiums shall be due upon delivery of "policy, and if not *paid within forty days after the close of the " calendar month* in which the insurance takes effect, notice of can- " cellation required by the Standard Policy shall be forthwith issued, " and if the premium is not paid within five days thereafter, the " policy shall be cancelled."

POLICIES ISSUED ON CREDIT AND WITHOUT QUESTION

If, after that time, the policy remain unpaid, a cancellation notice is usually issued. Companies have the option of cancelling policies after giving five days' previous notice in writing; but in the course of this investigation, ample time was given on most policies issued.

It will thus be seen that insurance is issued not only without question but " without price " for the time being. A prospective " fire bug " need not hesitate to apply for insurance simply because he lacks the price of the premium. Even in districts where ratings are high, policies are issued without any previous payment or investigation.

The only questions asked were of a perfunctory character, owing to the fact that the application was made " directly " and not through an agent. Most questions put to applicants who obtained insurance on behalf of the Fire Department arose simply from curiosity, owing to the fact that the insurance was not taken out through an agent. None of the questions hinged on what the household effects actually consisted of; or on the nature of the risk on which insurance was desired.

$10,500 OF INSURANCE ON $3.44 WORTH OF PROPERTY

For instance, in the " fire bug " district itself no difficulty was experienced in obtaining $10,500 worth of insurance on the $3.44 worth of " effects " placed in the flat at 239 East 101st street. The owners of this " household furniture " who had what might be considered an " insurable interest " therein were the following persons: Acting Chief William Guerin, Head of the Bureau of Fire Prevention, owned one chair—value 81c; Assistant Fire Marshal Herman W. de Malignon was the possessor of one gas heater—value $1; First-grade Fireman Washington S. Howe owned a chair, value 81c, and a pair of window curtains, worth 48c; another Assistant Fire Marshal—Montgomery Wade—owned one cuspidor for which he paid 9c; while W. B. Northrop, temporary Inspector, Bureau of Fire Prevention, laid claim to a piece of rubber tubing worth 25c.

On this amount of property, value $3.44, owned by the persons above mentioned, the following insurance policies in the companies named below were obtained:

COMPANIES ISSUING POLICIES

Date	Name of Company	Agent or Broker	No .of Policy	Premium	Amount
1912					
Feb. 19	Northwestern National of Milwaukee	J. H. Whittle	50051	$4.00	$1,000
Feb. 22	*Liverpool & London & Globe*	F. E. Jillson	9473479	10.00	1,000
Mar. 1	Caledonian	Limbach & Behning, managers	2319243	6.00	1,000
Mar. 28	Home Ins. Co., N. Y.	Joerns & French	369840	2.00	500
Mar. 29	Sun Ins. Office	U. S. Branch of Head Office	8513024	2.00	500
April 1	Germania	Uptown Office	616941	2.50	500
April 2	London & Lancashire Fire	N. Y. Office	8226474	2.00	500
April 2	Newark Fire	W. B. Ogden & Son.	11785	2.00	500
April 2	Norwich Union Fire of Norwich, Eng.	U. S. Office	6497839	2.00	500
April 3	Nat'l Union, Pittsburgh	F. S. James & Co.	27324	2.00	500
April 3	*Liverpool & London & Globe*	Starkweather & Shepley	9274582	2.00	500
April 3	Hartford Fire	N. Y. Office	578525	2.00	500
April 4	Continental	Home Office, N. Y.	A113604	2.00	500
April 4	Royal Exchange of London	Wm. Goodman	3876744	2.00	500
April 4	Williamsburgh City	N. Y. Office	1014410	3.00	500
April 5	American Ins. Co. of Newark	Wallace Reid	1552118	2.00	500
April 8	*Liverpool & London & Globe*	Forman & Herman.	9275481	3.00	500
May 14	Granite State Fire Ins. Co. of Portsmouth, N. H.	Benedict & Benedict.	851460	2.00	500

TOTAL VALUE OF PROPERTY, $3.44.
TOTAL INSURANCE THEREON $10,500
TOTAL PREMIUM CHARGED, $52.

NOTE—Companies in italics duplicated their insurance by issuing additional policies at the same address.

The foregoing statement shows the total amount of insurance secured on the $3.44 worth of property located at 239 East 101st Street; in a neighborhood of dubious character.

It will be seen that the rates vary considerably among the different companies. As to this variation of rate, a somewhat interesting letter was received by Assistant Fire Marshal Wade in reference to the policy of $1,000 applied for in the Liverpool & London & Globe Company. Application was made for insurance in the English company mentioned, but the agent through whom it was applied for offered to substitute for the Liverpool & London & Globe another company, the Western Assurance Company of Toronto, at "just one-half the Liverpool & London & Globe's rate." The agent, Mr. Frank E. Jillson, wrote the following letter:

COPY

Fire & Marine

THE WESTERN ASSURANCE COMPANY, TORONTO, CANADA

Hon. Geo. A. Cox, Pres.
W. B. Meikle, Gen. Man.
John Sime, Assist. Gen. Man.

Frank E. Jillson, Branch Manager
Room 212, 1511 3d Ave., cor.
85th St., New York City.

New York, March 2, 1912.

Mr. MONTGOMERY WADE,
239 East 101st Street,
New York City.

DEAR SIR:

Referring to your order for $1,000 insurance in the Liverp[illegible] & London & Globe Insurance Company covering household furnitur[illegible] at the above location, I wish to advise you that I have the policy in my office, but this company would not accept your risk at a less rate than 1% per annum, or $10.00 premium for one year. Therefore I took the liberty of placing the same in the Western Assurance Company at 50c per annum, or a premium of $5.00, just one-half the Liverpool & London & Globe's rate, and enclose you the policy herewith. If this policy is acceptable to you, kindly send me check as per the enclosed bill; or, on the other hand, if you still wish the Liverpool & London & Globe policy, kindly call here with the enclosed policy and I will give you the policy in the other company.

Yours very truly,
(signed) FRANK E. JILLSON,
Branch Manager.

It is somewhat singular to note that, though Mr. Jillson advises that the Liverpool & London & Globe company "*would not accept the risk* at a less rate than 1%, or $10 premium for one year," *the identical company*, through another agent—Messrs. Starkweather & Shepley, on April 3, 1912, *issued policy No.* 9274582 on *the same property at the same address* at the rate of $2 for $500 worth of insurance; or at the rate of $4 per $1,000; *and again*, on April 3d, through Messrs. Foreman & Herman, *issued policy No.* 9275481, at the rate of $3 for $500 worth of insurance, or at the rate of $6 per $1,000.

There seems to be considerable flexibility of rates among different companies. It will be noticed that several companies wrote the risk at $2 for $500 worth of insurance, while others charged rates considerably higher.

EASE WITH WHICH POLICIES WERE OBTAINED

Some difficulty was encountered by those who obtained the various policies for the Fire Department, owing to the fact that, not infrequently, the same agents represented several different companies; and it was thought that these agents might look with suspicion upon several different persons securing policies on the same property at the same address.

If "fire bugs" intended to burn up their property, it would seem that they would at once arouse suspicion if applying for $10,500 worth of insurance on the same property. Despite the fact, however, that several policies were issued by the same agents on this property, no inference seems to have been drawn. *Parties applying for insurance do not have to be known in any way.*

Out of all companies issuing policies on this property in 101st Street—16 in all—only one, the London & Lancashire Fire Insurance Company, issued a prompt cancellation notice through its Secretary, E. E. Pearce. The premium on this policy had been paid on April 2d—$2 for $500 worth of insurance—policy No. 8226474—and though the company cancelled the policy by notice served April 17, 1912, it failed to return the $2 paid by way of premium. It is true, no demand was made for the return of the premium; nor was the policy relinquished. Where a policy is cancelled within 15 days after issuance, the premium might have been returned as a matter of equity. Had incendiaries desired to take advantage of the policy issued by the London & Lancashire Company, they would have had ample time to do so in the 15 days' grace allowed before the cancellation of the policy.

As a matter of fact, though the London & Lancashire Fire Insurance Company's agent promptly issued a cancellation notice, he failed to return the premium; and, therefore, the policy was never adequately cancelled. The policy is now in possession of the Fire Department.

CHAPTER III.

More Policies Issued on Worthless Property—Further Instances of Careless Methods of Insurance Companies in Granting Policies—Insurance Experts Make Damaging Admissions—Companies Take "Over-Hazardous" Business if Paid to do so.

AFTER obtaining $10,500 worth of insurance on the "property" located at 239 East 101st Street, the effects were removed to 69 West 101st Street in order to ascertain whether rates on the west side of the city would be different from those on the east side; and also further to investigate the matter of the issuance of policies without previous inspection.

Much difficulty was experienced in obtaining rooming accommodation for the brief period of a month or two; particularly in view of the fact that no furniture to speak of was moved into the premises at any of the addresses named.

Previous inquiry of the janitor on the part of the insurance companies or their agents would have revealed the fact that no adequate amount of furniture had been carried into the premises. It is true that one or two of the companies did send a man up to the place to "look it over"; but with a single exception all these alleged inspectors took little trouble to ascertain the true facts in the case; and none insisted upon actually seeing the contents of the premises. One or two applicants from the Fire Department suggested that it might be well for the company to send someone to look over the property; but this offer was not taken up; and, invariably, the policy, or a "binder"—a covering note until policy could be written up—was given to the applicant without hesitation.

On the $3.44 worth of property installed in the new premises at 69 West 101st Street—for which a rental of $18 per month was paid—the following policies were issued by the companies named below:

MORE COMPANIES ISSUE POLICIES

Date	Name of Company	Agent or Broker	No. of Policy	Premium	Amount
1912					
April 16	Queens Ins. Co.	Home Office, N. Y.	29156	$2.00	$1,000
April 16	Northern Assurance of London	N. Y. Office	170924	2.00	1,000
April 16	Ins. Co. State of Penn.	N. Y. Office	155388	2.00	1,000
April 16	Hanover of N. Y.	Home Office	784024	2.00	1,000
April 16	*Ins. Co. of North America.*	J. M. Talbot & Co.	695441	2.00	1,000
April 16	City of N. Y. Ins. Co.	Home Office	37678	2.00	1,000
April 16	*Commercial Union Assurance Co. of London, Eng.*	N. Y. Office	6576464	2.00	1,000
April 17	Scottish Union & Nat'l Ins. Co. of Edinburgh	J. G. Hilliard	4568670	2.00	1,000

Continued next page.

Date	Name of Company	Agent or Broker	No. of Policy	Premium	Amount
April 17	Law Union & Rock Ins. Co. of London	Hall & Henshaw	1007482	$2.00	$1,000
April 17	Fire Association of Philadelphia	Kelly & Fuller	398580	2.00	1,000
April 18	London Assurance Corporation	U. S. Branch	3789563	2.00	1,000
April 18	German-American Ins. of N. Y.	Zieme & Hallett	737722	2.00	1,000
April 18	Fidelity-Phenix of New York	Newman & McBain	320692	2.00	1,000
April 18	Commonwealth Ins. Co. of N. Y.	Home Office	1220908	2.00	1,000
April 18	Atlas Assur. Co. of London, Eng.	N. Y. Office	6514286	2.00	1,000
April 18	Buffalo German Ins. Co.	F. H. Ross	180159	2.00	1,000
April 20	Palatine Ins. Co. of London, Eng.	Major A. White	58039	2.00	1,000
April 20	Mechanics Ins. Co. of Philadelphia	Wallace Reid	331773	2.00	1,000
April 23	Niagara of N. Y.	Home Office	641835	2.00	1,000
April 23	Firemans Fund of San Francisco	Wm. Goodman	297955	2.00	1,000
April 23	Phoenix Assurance of London	N. Y. Office	110411	2.00	1,000
April 24	*Connecticut Fire of Hartford*	E. Hall & Co.	283909	2.00	1,000
April 24	North River Ins. Company	Crum & Forster	1555052	2.00	1,000
April 24	Orient Ins. Co., Hartford, Conn.	Withers & Mills	617354	2.00	1,000
April 24	*Ins. Co. of North America.*	J. M. Talbot & Co.	695856	2.00	1,000
April 24	Boston Ins. Co.	Kelly & Fuller	1151592	2.00	1,000
April 24	Agricultural Ins. Co. of Watertown, N. Y.	J. H. Whittle	664487	2.00	1,000
April 24	Albany Ins. Co.	Schmidt & Donahue	16861	2.00	1,000
April 30	German Alliance Ins. Co. of N. Y.	Wm. Sohmer	257411	2.00	1,000
April 30	*Commercial Union Assurance Co. of London*	N. Y. Office	9500167	2.00	1,000
April 30	Citizens Fire Ins. Co., Charlestown, W. Va.	N. Y. Office	19318	2.00	1,000
April 30	*Connecticut Fire Ins. Co.*	W. S. Brown & Co.	283941	2.00	1,000
April 30	County Fire Ins. Co. of Phila.	A. B. Mills	531055	2.00	1,000
April 30	Royal Ins. Co. of Liverpool	Hy. Feldman & Son	972765	2.00	1,000
April 30	Concordia Fire Ins. of Milwaukee, Wis.	Lockwood Bros.	8857	2.00	1,000
May 1	Nat'l Ben Franklin Ins. of Pittsburg	R. D. Schell & Son	331849	2.00	1,000
May 1	Ins. Co. No. America	O'Brien & O'Brien	169469	2.00 (N.P.)	1,000
May 1	California Ins. Co. of San Francisco	J. G. Hilliard	559124	2.00	1,000
May 1	Century Ins. Co. of Scotland. (Risk declined—see letter)	H. W. Brown & Co.	Binder	.....	1,000
May 2	German-American Fire Ins. Co. of Baltimore, Md.	Hall & Henshaw	301398	2.00	1,000
May 2	Caledonian American Ins. Co.	Withers & Mills	134771	2.00	1,000

Continued next page.

Date	Name of Company	Agent or Broker	No. of Policy	Premium	Amount
May 2	Central National, Chicago, Ill.	Whilden & Hancock.	572082	$2.00	$1,000
May 2	Citizens of Mo.	Crum & Forster.	1085	2.70	1,000
May 2	Calumet Ins. Co. of Chicago.	F. S. James.	286234	2.00	1,000
May 4	American Fire Ins. Co.	Short & Co.	79612	5.00 (3 yrs.)	1,000
May 6	Greenwich Ins. Co. of New York.	Benedict & Benedict.	973	2.00	1,000
May 6	Detroit Fire & Marine.	H. Herrick.	39433	2.00	1,000
May 8	Hamburg-Bremen Fire Ins.	V. Freund & Son.	1928	2.00	1,000
May 8	Glens Falls Ins. Co., Glen Falls, N. Y.	Benedict & Benedict.	22807	2.00	1,000
	TOTAL POLICIES ON 69 WEST 101st STREET				$49,000
April 19	Newark Fire Ins. Co. on 101 West 69th Street (wrong address)	W. B. Ogden & Son.	11938	2.40	1,000
					$50,000

NOTE—Companies in italics duplicated their insurance by issuing additional policies at the same address.

By a singular oversight in the last policy on above list the figures of the address became transposed; and instead of issuing the policy on 69 West 101st Street, it was made out on 101 West 69th Street. It will be noticed that a slightly higher rate was charged. This was stated at the time to be due to the fact that the flat was over a store. No inspection of the furniture or premises was made other than consultation of an insurance map, the policy being issued simply upon payment of the premium—$2.40.

$60,500 INSURANCE ON WORTHLESS EFFECTS.

Altogether, on this address in West 101st Street, $49,000 of insurance in 42 different companies was obtained; while on the same "household effects" at East 101st Street, the sum of $10,500 of insurance was issued in the form of 18 different policies, with $1,000 at a wrong address where there were no "effects" at all, and where the applicant had not even rented an apartment, making a total insurance of $60,500 in both East and West 101st Street, and 101 West 69th Street, in 58 companies, several of them issuing more than one policy on the selfsame property.

As will be noticed by glancing through the lists, some companies, *The Liverpool & London & Globe; the Insurance Company of North America; the Commercial Union Assurance of London; the Connecticut Fire Insurance Company, issued duplicate policies at the same address,* no questions being asked.

Members of the Fire Department were thus able to obtain, with no difficulty other than the time taken up in making the application, a duplication of their original policies on the same furniture from the same companies. Had any of these companies taken the trouble to perform any sort of inspection, they would have ascertained that little furniture existed on the premises—and it is doubtful if it would have been possible to obtain $60,500 *worth of insurance on* $3.44 *worth of property.*

Dividing up the "insurable interest" of the persons who applied for these policies at the addresses given, including that issued at the wrong address, it might be stated that the following amounts of insurance were issued on the articles mentioned below:

Name of Article	Value	Amount of Insurance Issued on Same.
1 cuspidor	$0 09	$10,083 33
1 chair	81	10,083 33
1 chair	81	10,083 33
1 gas heater	1 00	10,083 33
1 rubber tube	25	10,083 33
Lace curtains	48	10,083 35
Total Value of Property	$3 44	$60,500 00 Total Insurance

One company alone attempted to make an inspection and sent a man, on two occasions, to the premises. After he had made some inquiries—doubtless ascertaining the small amount of property moved into the flat—he refused to issue the policy. This was the British American Assurance Company.

Another company, the Century Insurance Company of Scotland, issued a temporary insurance, or "binder," on May 1, 1912, but subsequently cancelled same. One or two other companies refused to issue policies on the East 101st Street address.

However, all companies mentioned on above lists issued policies with practically no inquiry whatever, and the policies are now in possession of the Fire Department, together with numbers of other policies issued on property at other addresses described subsequently in the course of this report.

THE ONE FACT THAT STANDS OUT IS THIS: UPWARDS OF 135 POLICIES WERE ISSUED BY FIRE INSURANCE COMPANIES DOING BUSINESS IN THIS CITY TO APPLICANTS WHOM THEY DID NOT KNOW; ON PROPERTY WHICH THEY TOOK NO TROUBLE TO INSPECT; AND THIS IN SPITE OF THE RECOMMENDATION OF THE LEGISLATIVE JOINT COMMITTEE OF THIS STATE TO THE SPECIFIC EFFECT THAT "WHEN AN APPLICATION FOR A POLICY IS RECEIVED BY AN AGENT HE SHOULD TAKE STEPS TO SATISFY HIMSELF THAT THE RISK IS A DESIRABLE ONE." (See report of the Joint Committee of the Senate and Assembly of the State of New York Appointed to Investigate Corrupt Practices in Connection with Legislation and the Affairs of Insurance Companies other than those doing Life Insurance Business, page 35.)

INSURANCE COMPANY METHODS ENCOURAGE ARSON

If inspection were carried out in all cases, large numbers of policies would have to be declined. Still, it were far better that companies should lose this business than that so much encouragement should be given to the commission of crime.

THE GREAT EASE WITH WHICH INSURANCE POLICIES ARE OBTAINED BEARS DIRECTLY UPON THE QUESTION OF ARSON. THE REFUSAL OF THE COMPANIES TO INSURE DOUBTFUL "RISKS" WOULD AUTOMATICALLY CHECK A LARGE PERCENTAGE OF THIS PHASE OF CRIMINAL ENTERPRISE.

Doubtful risks are accepted by the companies, however, without question when these risks are presented by agents or brokers from whom they may expect a large volume of preferred business. This was admitted by several insurance officials during the course of the Legislative inquiry into the methods of Fire Insurance Companies, already referred to. Among others, John H. Stoddart, general agent for the New York Underwriters Agency, representing several important companies, in his testimony on November 30, 1910, made the following answers to the question given below:

Question. Ordinarily the companies are not looking for poor risks, are they? Answer. No.

Q. And they want to stay away from them; the extra-hazardous class? A. *That depends upon the rate.* You can write extra-hazardous risks as any other kind *if you get enough to pay for them.*

Q. As a fact, they do carry poor risks? A. Yes.

Q. And isn't it a fact that *they do that for the reason that if they would not take that class of risks from the agent they would not get that preferred business?* A. *There is an element in that.* (See Legislative report, page 1442.)

After securing $60,500 worth of insurance in policies on "effects" at the two addresses in 101st Street and at the wrong address, 101 West 69th Street, it was decided to remove the furniture, give up the flat and secure another address, at 203 East 77th Street. As none of the companies had taken the trouble to make actual inspection before issuing policies, there seemed no necessity for placing any of the $3.44 worth of effects in the new apartment; which was a three-roomed one on the second floor, under a rental of $15 per month. It was taken on May 16, 1912.

In order, however, to have some "insurable interest" in the place, and so that it might not be absolutely bare in case some enterprising agent might take a notion to perform the rare task of "inspection," the following articles were bought and placed in the flat:

	Value.
2 picture frames	10c.
1 nickel-plated soap dish	10c.
	20c.

The above was the total value of the "property" placed in the apartment mentioned. Application was now made among the insurance companies from which policies had not already been secured, and the following policies were obtained:

POLICIES SECURED ON 20c WORTH OF "PROPERTY"

Date	Name of Company	Agent or Broker	No. of Policy	Premium	Amount
1912					
May 15	Teutonia of Allegheny, Pa.	Kelly & Fuller	315343	$2. NP*	$1,000
May 15	Teutonia of New Orleans	M. J. Cremins	404908	2. NP	1,000
May 15	Sun of New Orleans	Hall & Henshaw	979833	2. NP	1,000
May 16	Springfield Fire & Marine	Chas. G. Smith	433386	2. NP	1,000
May 16	Security Ins. Co., New Haven	J. G. Hilliard	317409	2. NP	1,000
May 16	St. Paul Fire & Marine	Foreman & Herman	108543	2. Pd	1,000
May 16	Stuyvesant Ins. Co.	Head Office	932282	2. NP	1,000
May 16	Union of Buffalo	Crum & Forster	240459	2. NP	1,000

Continued next page.

Date	Name of Company	Agent or Broker	No. of Policy	Premium	Amount
1912					
May 16	United Firemen's of Philadelphia..........	Newman & McBain..	18893	2. NP	1,000
May 16	Rhode Island of Providence................	Starkweather & Shepley..........	211479	2. NP	1,000
May 16	Northern Ins. Co., N. Y..	Williard S. Brown...	118934	2. NP	1,000
May 16	Pelican Assur. of N. Y....	William Sohmer.....	277581	2. Pd	1,000
May 20	U. S. Underwriters'...... UNDERWRITTEN BY North River Co. Nassau Fire Ins. Co. Empire City. U. S. Fire Ins. Co.	Crum & Forster.....	67521	2. NP	1,000
May 20	Delaware of Phila........	Newman & McBain..	543406	2 NP	1,000
May 20	Pacific of N. Y..........	Head Office.........	29141	2. NP	1,000
May 20	Westchester Fire Ins. Co..	Home Office........	264453	2. NP	1,000
May 20	Union Fire Ins. Co. of Paris, France.........	Starkweather & Shepley..........	750634	2. NP	1,000
May 20	Western Ins. Co. of Pittsburg.................	Duross Co..........	738596	2. NP	1,000
May 20	Prussian Nat'l of Stettin, Germany.............	J. G. Hilliard.......	1698817	2. NP	1,000
May 21	Old Colony of Boston....	Kelly & Fuller......	428444	2. NP	1,000
May 21	Commerce of Albany.....	W. B. Ogden & Son..	7810	2. NP	1,000
May 21	Mechanics & Traders of New Orleans..........	W. B. Ogden & Son..	258988	2. NP	1,000
May 22	Pennsylvania of Philadelphia..............	Julius W. Helbing...	533174	2. NP	1,000
May 22	The Capitol, Concord, N. H................	Tallman & Sears....	362867	2. NP	1,000
May 22	Pittsburg Fire Ins.......	A. B. Mills.........	26134	2. Pd	1,000
May 23	New Brunswick of New Brunswick, N. J.......	Frank E. Jillson.....	449428	2. NP	1,000
May 23	New Jersey of Newark...	Whilden & Hancock.	58455	2. NP	1,000
May 25	Phoenix of Hartford.....	Chas. G. Smith.....	160700	2. NP	1,000
May 25	Yorkshire of York, Eng...	W. S. Brown & Co...	57623	2. NP	1,000
May 29	Connecticut Fire of Hartford................	O'Brien & O'Brien...	284694	2. NP	1,000
May 29	North British & Mercantile.................	U. S. Branch........	1356944	2.	1,000
June 3	Milwaukee Mechanics'...	T. Y. Brown........	112692	2. NP	1,000
June 4	Hartford Fire Ins........ (Through Underwriters' Agency, N. Y.)	....	755176	2. NP	1,000
June 5	Lumber Ins. Co., N. Y...	Newman & McBain..	846612	2. NP	1,000
June 5	Nationale of Paris.......	Starkweather & Shepley..........	951551	2. NP	1,000
June 5	Reliance of Phila........	M. J. Cremins......	118940	2. NP	1,000
June 5	Virginia Fire & Marine of Richmond...........	Hall & Henshaw....	941568	2. NP	1,000
June 5	American Union Fire Ins. of Phila.............	Whilden & Hancock.	150852	2. NP	1,000
June 5	Dutchess Fire Ins. of Poughkeepsie, N. Y....	Crum & Forster.....	113454	2. NP	1,000
June 5	American Central of St. Louis...............	J. G. Hilliard.......	842920	2. NP	1,000

TOTAL INSURANCE ON 20c WORTH OF "PROPERTY" AT 203 EAST 77TH STREET, MANHATTAN.......... $40,000

* NP means Not Paid.

It will thus be seen that 40 insurance companies issued $40,000 in policies on property at 203 East 77th Street; the total value of this property being 20c. Taking the "insurable interest" of those applying for the policies, it appears that the following persons received policies on the articles named below:

Article	Value	Person Applying	Policies Issued Amount
1 picture frame	5c	Hugh L. Hannighan	$20,000
1 picture frame	5c	Rudolph Dillman	12,000
1 soap dish	10c	Eugene McCaffery	8,000
TOTAL VALUE	20c	TOTAL INSURANCE	$40,000

NEW QUARTERS TAKEN AND MORE INSURANCE OBTAINED

The above mentioned "effects" were, on June 14, 1912, removed by the persons owning the "insurable interest" in them.

An apartment at 220 East 36th Street was then secured. It was not considered necessary to install any property whatever in the place as the possibility of "inspection" seemed very remote. However, in order to have a slight "insurable interest" in the flat, the following persons placed in it these effects:

Person Insuring	Article	Value	Insurance
Gustave R. Moje	1 looking glass	10c	
Hugh J. Joyce	1 china fruit dish	5c	
Richard P. Shea	1 tea strainer	5c	
		20c	$19,000

All persons mentioned above are employees of the Fire Department, but none was known as such to insurance companies or their agents.

The following policies were issued on this property by the companies named below:

POLICIES ISSUED ON FLAT AT 220 EAST 36TH STREET

Date	Name of Company	Agent or Broker	No. of Policy	Premium	Amount
1912					
Aug. 2	Fidelity-Phenix of New York	Newman & McBain	323258	$2. NP	$1,000
Aug. 2	Nat'l of Hartford	F. S. James & Co.	775312	2. NP	1,000
Aug. 2	Am. Ins. of Newark	M. J. Cremins	1556222	2. NP	1,000
Aug. 2	Svea of Gothenburg, Sweden	A. B. Mills	571740	2. Pd	1,000
Aug. 2	Equitable Fire & Marine, Providence, R. I.	Hall & Henshaw	459902	2. NP	1,000
Aug. 2	Glens Falls, N. Y.	T. Y. Brown & Co.	24736	2. NP	1,000
Aug. 2	Scottish Union & Nat'l of Edinburgh	J. G. Hilliard	4572696	2. NP	1,000
Aug. 2	Dubuque Fire & Marine of Dubuque, Iowa	W. L. Perrin & Son	917843	2. NP	1,000

Continued next page.

Date	Name of Company	Agent or Broker	No. of Policy	Premium	Amount
Aug. 9	Dixie Fire, Greensboro, N. C.	Newman & McBain	390454	$2. NP	$1,000
Aug. 9	Lumbermen's Ins. Co. of Philadelphia	J. G. Hilliard	40436	2. NP	1,000
Aug. 9	Merchants' Fire Ins., Denver, Colorado	W. L. Perrin & Son	1821	2. NP	1,000
Aug. 9	Nassau of Brooklyn	Crum & Forster	781284	2. NP	1,000
Aug. 16	People's Nat'l of Philadelphia	Newman & McBain	521521	2. NP	1,000
Aug. 16	Nat'l Lumber of Buffalo, N. Y.	Crum & Forster	120480	2. NP	1,000
Aug. 16	Providence Washington of Providence, R. I.	Wm. Dinsmore & Son	244473	2. NP	1,000
Aug. 16	Farmers' of York, Pa.	W. L. Perrin & Son	101693	2. NP	1,000
Aug. 16	German-American of Pennsylvania	Whilden & Hancock	199509	2. Pd	1,000
Aug. 16	Standard Fire of Hartford	J. G. Hilliard	36582	5. 3 yr.	1,000
Aug. 30	Northwestern Nat'l of Milwaukee	Jno. K. Bainbridge	51949	2. NP	1,000

TOTAL INSURANCE ON: 1 Looking Glass; 1 China Fruit Dish; 1 Tea Strainer—WORTH 20c.................. $19,000

Taking the totals of the two lists, this makes an insurance of $59,000 *on articles costing* 40c.

THE FIRE BUG AND HIS "PROOF OF LOSS"

Insurance officials argue that, in order to collect insurance on such articles, "proof of loss" would have to be submitted. For the professional fire bug, the "proof of loss" matter presents no difficulties. His system of operation includes knowledge of where he can obtain *ample supplies of false invoices and fake affidavits* "proving" that the goods were regularly purchased. In some cases, goods and furniture that have done duty at other fires are previously placed in the premises; and there are persons quite willing, for a share of the profits, to supply, after the fire, all necessary "proofs of loss" that may be required.

In the Bertolino and other cases—reference to which will be found in subsequent chapters of this report—not only were false "proofs of loss" submitted; but in one case—the Sam Brant affair—the fire bug had no property whatever on the premises; and yet, if his plan had been successful, he would have been able to secure large amounts of insurance from the companies. (See p. 68.)

EASE OF OBTAINING POLICIES

It has been amply demonstrated in the foregoing sections of this report that *any amount of insurance may be obtained by almost anybody*—either "directly" or through agents or brokers—*from practically* ALL *Fire Insurance Companies doing business in Greater New York.*

The ease with which this insurance was obtained, and the utter lack of caution on the part of the companies or their agents—even in hazardous districts—will afford an intimation of how would-be incendiaries readily provide themselves with insurance policies which form the necessary incentives to their crimes.

In addition to the policies enumerated above, the following ones were secured on 12c worth of "property" at 208 East 73d Street:

Date 1912	Name of Company	Name of Agent	No. of Policy	Premium	Amount
Sept. 18	People's Nat'l of Philadelphia	Newman & McBain	521983	$2. NP*	$1,000
Sept. 18	German Fire of Wheeling, West Va.	J. G. Hilliard	204462	2. NP	1,000
Sept. 18	Imperial of Denver	Bainbridge & White	(Binder)	2. NP	1,000
Sept. 18	Ohio Farmers Ins. Co.	W. L. Perrin & Son	N2480	2. NP	1,000
Oct. 7	Firemans of Newark	Forman & Herman	2033172	2. Pd	1,000
Oct. 7	Western Ins. of Toronto, Can.	Major White	5693950	2. NP	1,000
Oct. 11	Etna of Hartford	Benedict & Benedict	(Binder)	2. NP	1,000
Oct. 11	Millers' Nat'l of Chicago	W. L. Perrin & Son	103045	2. NP	1,000

TOTAL INSURANCE ON 12c WORTH OF PROPERTY... $8,000

*NP means Not Paid.

The above insurance—$8,000—was granted on the following articles: 1 knife; 1 fork; 1 salt-shaker—total value 12c, the "insurable interest" in which was owned by the following employees of the Fire Department: Lieutenant John H. Corr; Lieutenant F. H. McGuinness, and Fireman Daniel L. Foley.

To summarize the previous lists of insurance on articles of practically no value:

RECAPITULATION

INSURANCE ON ARTICLES VALUED AT	$3.44	$59,500
" " " " "	.20c....	40,000
" " " " "	.20c....	19,000
" " " " "	.12c....	8,000
" " " " "	.00c....	1,000
TOTAL INSURANCE ON ARTICLES WORTH	$3.96	$127,500

CHAPTER IV.

Persons Who Benefit From Having Fires—Trades in Which Most Fires Occur—Bad Business Increases Incendiarism—Financial Conditions Influence Number of Fires—Insurance Companies and the Famous Bertolino Case—Judge Swann Says Companies "Openly Invite Crime."

"Were there no fires, there would be no insurance business; and, on the "other hand, the greater the fire damage, the greater the turn-over, out of "which insurance companies make profits. Speaking to-night as Manager "of a Fire Insurance Company, I say we cannot make profits for our share- "holders without fires. And, further, that within certain well-defined limits, "we welcome fires."

THE above outspoken sentiments are said to express the views of the Manager of the Scottish Union and National Fire Insurance Company of Edinburgh in a speech which he is alleged to have made not long ago before the Insurance and Actuarial Association of Glasgow. This candid admission may be taken in connection with the statement of the New York Board of Fire Underwriters; that "37.6 per cent. in number of incurred losses during the year 1911 were from assured who have had previous losses."

Though many concerns in New York to-day have had numbers of "previous" fires—one prominent firm in the shirt waist line having had nine—on which they have collected ample insurance, their ability to obtain more insurance remains unimpaired. Insurance companies make few inquiries save as to the ability of the assured to pay premiums.

It has been shown, in a former section of this report, how easy it is for individuals to obtain insurance on household effects. It goes without saying, therefore, that business firms experience no difficulty in obtaining not only their full amount of insurance but as much over-insurance as they are willing to pay for. The fact that certain firms are addicted to having fires does not deter them from obtaining whatever insurance they require. Numbers of firms are to-day doing business in Greater New York whose fortunes have been literally built up by the "previous" fire insurance they have succeeded in collecting.

Such facts as these make the operation of gangs of fire bugs profitable to all parties concerned—not even excepting insurance companies.

TRADES IN WHICH MOST FIRES OCCUR

Before examining statistics relating to Trade Fires in New York City, it must be stated that no reflection is intended upon the hundreds of honorable firms engaged in these industries. The Fire Department investigation only covers such of these firms as have definitely placed themselves under suspicion.

An examination of the 14,574 fires in Greater New York during 1911 reveals the fact that many individual firms in these trades have acquired the "fire habit." Among these are certain firms in the SHIRT WAIST INDUSTRY. Inspection of individual reports dealing with this class of fire shows that in 69 per cent. of instances, the causes of these fires were unknown; or, officially reported to the Fire Department as "Not Ascertained."

Many of these fires are undoubtedly of incendiary origin, though it is extremely difficult to obtain actual evidence of that fact. The Fire Marshal, while strongly suspecting such fires to be suspicious in character, lacks specific proof, and therefore lists them as cause "Not Ascertained."

Out of 49 fires in the SHIRT WAIST TRADE, as many as 34—or 69 per cent.—were found to be among the "Cause Not Ascertained" variety. Of the 15 remaining fires, the assigned causes are as follows: Pressing iron, 5 fires; benzine, 1; hot stove, 2; cigarette smoking, 3; carelessness, 1, and throwing match, 3.

Many of these firms are scandalously over-insured.

Another trade in which many individuals are over-insured and one among which more than 58 per cent. of the fires are "Not Ascertained"—is the CLOAK AND WOMEN'S SUIT BUSINESS. Here, out of 94 fires the causes of 55 were "Not Ascertained," while the ascertained causes among the balance were as follows: 2 were due to short circuited wires; 6 to pressing irons; 9 to lighted cigars and cigarettes; 1 to sparks from engine; 3 to gas jet; 1 to a hot coal; 1 to rubbish; 3 to defective wiring; 1 to turpentine, 10 to matches, and 2 are plainly indicated as "SUSPICIOUS."

The ease with which business firms in this and other trades obtain over-insurance, even after having numerous fires, is further evidence of the laxity, or worse, of insurance methods.

Another trade having a large proportion of fires which are of incendiary origin, is the FUR INDUSTRY. Here, out of 21 fires, 14—or more than 66 per cent.—were of "unknown cause."

In the HAT AND CAP INDUSTRY, out of 14 fires, no less than 10—more than 71 per cent.—were attributed to "Unknown cause"; and the amount of insurance was in almost every instance disproportionate to the interest involved.

REMARKABLE PERCENTAGES IN TRADE FIRES

Taking a list of trades at random, the percentages of "Not Ascertained" fires work out as follows:

Trades	Number of Fires	Not Ascertained	Per Cent.
Leather Goods	22	14	63
Cloaks and Women's Suits	94	55	58
Embroidery	32	21	65
Flowers and Feathers	14	7	50
Millinery	24	17	70
Novelties and Toys	19	15	78
Shirt Waists	49	34	69
Furs	21	14	66
Hats and Caps	14	10	71

Despite the fact that suspicious fires occur repeatedly in the trades mentioned, insurance companies take no extra precautions to inquire into character and standing of persons requiring insurance. Nor is the fact of many previous fires held against a business man—so far as the companies are concerned—provided the premium is paid and the location of the premises complies with the requirements of the Fire Insurance Exchange.

At the present moment, there is absolutely no "character test" in granting fire insurance; and the manner in which policies are issued to so-called "business" firms is quite on a par with that pursued in the granting of policies on household effects.

Taking what might be called "normal trades," other than the above, the general average of "Not Ascertained" fires works out in the neighborhood of about 30 per cent. In many trades, non-ascertainable causes run below 10 per cent.

Industries included in above lists, however, have "Not Ascertained" fires running as high as 78 per cent.; 71 per cent.; 66 per cent., and so on. The only general conclusion to be drawn from such facts is that *large numbers of fires which occur in these trades are of incendiary origin.*

FIRES TAKE PLACE WHEN BUSINESS IS BAD

This conclusion is confirmed by inquiry into the time of the year at which suspicious fires occur in such trades as SHIRT WAISTS, CLOAKS AND WOMEN'S SUITS, FURS, HATS AND CAPS, EMBROIDERY, MILLINERY, FLOWERS AND FEATHERS, and allied industries. Bad seasons, overstocking of goods, failure of salesmen to secure expected orders, invariably result in an abundance of "accidents"—*i. e.,* fires—among certain firms in the trades involved.

In the FUR TRADE, for instance, most fires occur in the spring of the year. This is because trade slacks down in these months; and some of the "business men" who deal in furs can then judge whether or not they have a chance of turning the corner with their stock. If not, they may—and often do— call in the good offices of the "fire syndicate," or someone else, to help them out with a fire. Or else, they "take a chance" and attempt to make the fire themselves. Inexperience sometimes land them in the toils of the Fire Marshal. The "expert" operator is usually too clever to be caught except through some unforeseen accident.

In the CLOAK AND SUIT TRADE there are many incendiary fires during the season of business depression. This is usually from September to December. Investigation shows that certain unscrupulous manufacturers in the cloak and suit trade deliberately set fire to their places of business as a direct result of bad market conditions caused by the Mississippi floods. In these instances customers in the flooded district had failed and collections were slow.

In the HAT AND CAP TRADE there are also incendiary fires, depending largely upon the market. Most HAT AND CAP FIRES occur from May to August. Many instances have come to light during the investigations following suspicious fires in this trade where an overstock of hats and caps has resulted unquestionably in an incendiary blaze.

In the MILLINERY AND FEATHER TRADE, a change of fashions will result in a number of fires. When willow plumes went out of style recently, there were large numbers of fires in this line. The same applies to the EMBROIDERY TRADE. It is largely dependent upon fashions. Any overstock of supplies held by certain people in these trades is repleted with fire "possibilities." *Incendiary fires occurring in many trades carried on in Greater New York depend largely upon market conditions.* This is amply proved by records compiled by the Fire Department.

LOW FINANCES INDUCE MAKING OF "BUSINESS FIRES"

Another extremely important factor—financial condition—exerts powerful influence upon the number of incendiary fires. Dishonest merchants whose bank balances are at the lowest ebb and who know not where to turn to avoid impending disaster, seek consolation in conflagration, so to speak.

As the Fire Marshal can tell from a study of seasonal trades, and fashion-dependent industries, just when fires might be expected; so scrutiny of Dun and Bradstreet reports will reveal the names of persons or companies who might logically be expected to have fires.

If reports of low finances were supplied at specific times to the Fire Department in all of above trades, there is little doubt that it would be possible to designate beforehand the very firms in whose premises fires would most likely occur.

It would be a decided advantage to the Fire Department to know where and when such fires would take place. Certain experiments have already been tried in the Fire Department to "warn" suspected people in some of these trades that they were under observation. For instance, uniformed men have been sent—for the purpose of ostensible "inspection"—to certain premises which, logically, might be expected to have fires—judging from their financial and trade condition and their past record. In many of these cases, fires have not occurred for the reason that the firms or individuals were aware of being watched.

A system of reports to the Fire Department of all firms having overstocks of goods in seasonal trades, or trades governed by changes of fashions, and which included a statement of financial standing during the period when fires might ordinarily be expected, would certainly act as a decided deterrent in the number of fires in the trades specified. *It is high time that these perennial "business" fires ceased.* They can only be stopped by giving powers to the Fire Department to inquire minutely into trade conditions and financial standing of certain firms and to require regularly certified statements from such firms whose past records show that they have already availed themselves of the advantages of over-insurance and repeated fires.

PLAIN DUTY OF INSURANCE COMPANIES

If Insurance Companies, before granting policies, took the trouble to ascertain financial conditions of individual firms they would be able to remove the temptation from a large number of firms and individuals who today are having fires as a matter of ordinary "business" procedure.

INSURANCE COMPANIES SHOULD ALSO TAKE MEASURES TO MAKE IT DIFFICULT FOR ALL WHO HAVE HAD PREVIOUS SUSPICIOUS FIRES TO OBTAIN INSURANCE. But, as long as it is openly stated by the companies that "37.6 per cent. of incurred losses are among assured who have had previous fires," the condition seems irremediable, so far as the insurance companies themselves are concerned.

THE LIBERAL ISSUE BY INSURANCE COMPANIES OF POLICIES TO BOTH INDIVIDUALS AND BUSINESS FIRMS, WITHOUT ANY PREVIOUS INQUIRY AS TO CHARACTER, OR INSPECTION AS TO RISK, IS ONE OF THE PRINCIPAL CAUSES OF INCENDIARISM.

To afford a concrete instance of the carelessness of insurance companies in granting business insurance, the case of Antonio Bertolino will be cited. This case, tried before Judge Edward Swann on February 2, 1912, in General Sessions, Manhattan, resulted in a conviction for arson in the third degree. The case attained considerable notoriety, owing to the scathing remarks of Judge Swann, directed against insurance methods.

THE BERTOLINO CASE

Bertolino was an Italian who kept a grocery at 507-509 Broome Street, Manhattan. He had followed many occupations, and had not been successful in any. At the time of the fire in question, he was very much embarrassed for funds and was on the point of failure. A few days prior to the fire he had given a check for $111.40 in payment for increased insurance policies on his store, but the check had been returned marked "insufficient funds." Bertolino's low financial status did not seem to arouse the suspicion of the insurance people to whom he gave this worthless check.

On the night of November 19, 1911, at 7.50 o'clock, fire was discovered in his place, and when the first fireman entered the premises at 7.52, the sound of a muffled explosion was heard. The fire made little headway and was soon extinguished, upon which it was discovered that a number of bladders filled with ether and benzine had been placed about the shop in such position that they would explode and burn out the store. Not only were many ether filled bladders, connected by inflammable trailers, found, but barrels full of oil had been placed in such position that they would burn readily.

Bertolino, to manufacture a plausible alibi, was, at the time of the blaze, attending a christening a few doors away from the scene of the fire.

With singular forethought, he had invited to this christening the very insurance agent from whom he had obtained his insurance and from whom he had secured an increase of his policies just before the fire. On November 6—13 days before the fire—Bertolino had increased his insurance from $2,000 to $5,400.

The stock which Bertolino had insured for the large amount here mentioned was not worth even the $2,000 which had been previously placed upon it. Much of the stock was not only unmerchantable, but actually decayed. The total value of the goods in the place was subsequently appraised at about $990.

In order to create an impression that he was doing a rushing business, Bertolino had, just previous to the fire, rented additional floor space, and had ostentatiously purchased from a friend a considerable quantity of a substance called "pignolia," which, on examination, proved to be rotten. Despite this display of prosperity, his balance in bank on the morning after the fire proved to be but $55.58. He produced a number of *"fake" invoices and receipted bills* to make good his claim for loss.

JUDGE SWANN ASKS PERTINENT QUESTIONS

During the course of this trial, which began January 23, and lasted ten days, ending February 2, 1912, Judge Swann took great interest in the matter of insurance and put some pertinent questions to the agent, who had handled Bertolino's insurance.

A portion of the testimony taken from the Court Record is as follows:

> Question by the Court—Did you inspect his goods in the store at the time you wrote his first policy? Answer. The idea of insurance is that you must prove your loss—Bertolino could just as well order $50,000 as $200—he must prove his loss.

Q. Or $100,000 (of insurance)? A. Yes, sir.

Q. In case of a loss, you let him fight it out afterwards? A. He must prove his loss with the companies. We would have adjusted his loss—but he must prove it.

Q. Let me get this plainly: Suppose, for instance, I should say I would like you to write me a policy for $8,000 on my furniture uptown, would you write the policy? Answer. We would place the policy, we don't write the policy.

Q. You would place it right off? A. Without a doubt, if the neighborhood was good—*without any inspection.*

Q. *Although I might not have* $50 *worth of furniture?* A. *Yes, that is true*—if you have a loss, you must prove it.

Q. And if I have a loss, I will have to prove what the loss was—suppose it was a total loss? A. You have to prove it.

Q. Suppose you go up there, and there was a nice good fire, and nothing but cinders left, how are you going to prove or disprove my affidavit that I have a loss of $8,000 worth of furniture?

This last question the witness was unable to answer satisfactorily, and the Judge put this further point:

> Q. Do you know whether the companies, or any of the companies, in this particular case, did anything to advise themselves or inform themselves as to the value of the stock that they were insuring? A. No, sir—the Home didn't go near it, and the Commonwealth didn't go near it.

(Bertolino's insurance was in the Home, Commonwealth and the Liverpool and London and Globe Companies.)

REPREHENSIBLE CONDUCT OF INSURANCE COMPANIES' AGENT

After the prosecution had begun, the agent approached the prisoner and suggested to him that if he would withdraw his claim against the companies, they would not bring action criminally. *The sole object of the companies in this case was to have their claims settled, and the matter of the public danger through the act of arson committed by Bertolino appeared of no moment whatever.*

Remarkably prompt action of the Fire Department in responding to this fire prevented what might have been one of the worst conflagrations which has ever visited New York. The district where the fire took place—Broome Street near West Broadway—is of particularly hazardous character; and a fire once under way in that section might lay lower New York in ashes. Not only was the granting of insurance in the Bertolino case an act of highly reprehensible character; but the attempt to obtain from him a release of claims against the companies throws a very ugly light upon the matter.

The Bertolino case became famous in the annals of arson trials owing to the facts brought out by the learned Judge during the course of the trial in relation to the responsibility of insurance companies. At the conclusion of the proceedings, there was an interesting colloquy among the Judge, Jury, and Assistant District Attorney, Mr. Charles P. Bostwick:

Among other things, the Judge said, regarding the fires which occurred in Greater New York during the previous year:

JUDGE SWANN'S OPINION ON ARSON

> "It is my private opinion that the majority of those fires are incendiary. * * * There was not any question but that this fire was incendiary, that it was all prepared, and we know, although we cannot put it in evidence, that *any man who wants a fire in the City of New York for a small consideration—my recollection is* $250, *paid to the syndicate—can have his house fired or his place fired in the most approved style known to those particular members of the syndicate.*
>
> "Of course that man is as guilty as the man who touches the match. We know these things occur. We know it occurs all the time—probably occurs every day; and, as I say, if we could be just a little constructive, as well as disposing of a particular case before us, we could put a stop to a great many of these incendiary fires."

In a letter to Fire Commissioner Johnson, written February 2, 1912—the day of the conclusion of the trial—Judge Swann had this to say concerning insurance companies:

> "THIS CASE BROUGHT OUT THE FACT THAT THE CUSTOM OF THE INSURANCE COMPANIES IN INSURING A STOCK OF MERCHANDISE FOR PRACTICALLY ANY AMOUNT DESIRED BY THE INSURED, WITHOUT MAKING ANY EFFORT TO DISCOVER THE PRIOR APPRAISAL OF THE MERCHANDISE, IS AN OPEN INVITATION TO MEN OF CRIMINAL INSTINCT TO COMMIT THE CRIME OF ARSON."

CHAPTER V.

Public Adjusters and Their Questionable Practices—How the Adjuster Gets Through the Fire Lines—"Padding" Claims After Fires—Adjusters and Fire Bugs Work Together—Dishonest Adjusters and Their Methods—Remedies for the Adjusting Evil.

> "Parties suffering loss by fire are particularly cautioned for their own safety not to make any agreement nor sign any paper relating to such loss until they have conferred with the office of the company insuring them."

THUS reads the "warning" of the New York Board of Fire Underwriters against a class of persons commonly known as "Public Adjusters." The function of the public adjuster is a peculiar one and is exercised in a peculiar manner.

It is the self-imposed duty of this functionary, immediately on the occurrence of a fire in any part of the metropolis, to hasten to the scene thereof, and to get in touch with the insured person affected by the fire. If the fire occur in a tenement house, the adjuster hunts for the occupant of the apartment and the insured "boarders," if any.

If the fire be of a "business" character, the head of the firm or firms is found.

Among public adjusters, the keenest competition prevails. Cases have been known where as many as ten public adjusters were seeking the same insured party at the same time; and one of them only succeeded in getting in touch with his client—or victim—by virtually kidnapping the assured and carrying him away in an automobile.

Ostensibly, public adjusters haunt the scene of fires for the purpose of performing the part of philanthropists looking solely after the interests of the assured; so that, by means of the superior technical knowledge of the adjuster, the assured may collect his full claim against the insurance companies covering the loss for which policies have been issued. Actually, they are influenced solely by motives of keen self-interest.

HOW ADJUSTERS ACT AT FIRES

Public adjusters, at a fire, attempt to obtain contracts with the assured, entitling the adjusters to sole charge of the collection of all insurance losses. Cases have been known where these adjusters have obtained as many as five separate contracts from assured persons immediately after fires, each contract promising 10 per cent. of the insurance money to the adjuster; the assured being thus compelled on settlement to give up fully 50 per cent. of his claim against the insurance companies. Certain of the more reputable companies absolutely refuse to deal with public adjusters, only transacting their business through brokers, or through the assured.

Several public adjusters are now under indictment for grand larceny and other charges, and not a few of them have by their practices brought the entire class of public adjusters into disrepute.

It must not be inferred, from what has been said, that all public insurance adjusters are engaged in dishonest practices; but it is only intended here to point to some of the questionable methods pursued by the more enterprising members of this fraternity, especially in cases where arson charges might arise. Doubtless there are in Greater New York many honest agents and adjusters; but we are not dealing with them.

The attempt is here made to show the connection between the incendiary and the adjuster, the latter acting as a very convenient intermediary between the fire bug and the insurance company. It is safe to say that if many incendiaries had to appear personally in the offices of insurance companies or of their accredited agents, and could not conceal themselves behind the crooked adjuster, the actual facts connected with many questionable fires would be revealed, and the companies refuse to pay such losses.

The usual form of contract obtained by adjusters after fires reads as follows:

> New York.....................19
>
> "To the Insurance Company interested; or whom it may concern: (name of assured)
>
> "Hereby retains (name of adjuster) to advise and assist in the adjustment of ...... loss by fire of (date) at (name of locality) and agrees to pay him for such services on presentation of first check, a fee of ...... per cent. of the amount of loss as adjusted, or otherwise recovered from the companies, hereby giving him a lien on all policies and papers connected with said loss to the extent of said fee and advances."

The usual amount claimed by the adjuster is 10 per cent. of whatever loss may be recovered from the companies. While this legal fee does not seem at all unreasonble for arranging all the papers, and transacting the business of collecting the money from an insurance company after a fire, the adjuster does not always content himself with his legal allowance. Instances are on record where he has taken as high as 50 per cent. of the amount paid by the company, and in many cases, even more.

PADDING THE INSURANCE CLAIM AFTER A FIRE

As the adjuster is permitted to take 10 per cent. of the total loss paid by the company, it is naturally to his interest that the loss should be as large as possible. Not infrequently, an adjuster will turn a $1,000 loss into one of $1,500 or more by his skillful manipulation of the inventory after the fire. His knowledge of the preparation of a claim is of great use to the assured, even in cases where the fire is of purely accidental character.

As public adjusters swarm to all fires, and endeavor to obtain contracts, and as the average insured person is wholly ignorant of the adjustment of claims, the function of the adjuster is, for the time being, a somewhat important one.

Few assured persons know that the employment of an adjuster is wholly unnecessary; or realize that they would obtain more from the company directly than by resorting to the tender mercies of an adjuster. However, the average assured person falls an easy victim to the wiles of the adjuster, and either consents to claiming more from the company than his actual fire-loss consists of, or else leaves the whole matter to the adjuster, who "fixes everything" and appropriates as large an amount of the loss paid as possible.

Adjusters resort to all sorts of tactics to reach their clients on the scene of a fire. Some have fire-line badges, others display badges of various descriptions—such as those of Building Inspectors or other officials—and not infrequently represent themselves as being employees of the Fire Department or of the Fire Patrol.

Usually, at a fire, considerable confusion prevails, and officers do not stop to examine the exact pattern of an adjuster's badge. Consequently, adjusters—by resorting to all sorts of questionable practices—experience little difficulty in getting through fire lines. Many adjusters have acquaintances among newspaper reporters or editors, from whom they obtain badges or cards which admit them past fire-lines. At crooked fires, the adjuster often represents himself as having a "pull" in the Fire Marshal's office. He even volunteers to coach the assured in the information he may be required to give the Fire Marshal should inquiry into the facts of the fire eventuate.

Advance information as to location of fires is readily obtained by adjusters. Some, through their newspaper connection obtain telephonic calls to all fires; others make it a practice to watch the signal boards outside engine houses in order to obtain alarm numbers. By carefully systematized efforts, adjusters secure immediate information concerning the location of any fire in the city, and they often reach the scene as quickly as the fire apparatus.

QUICK WORK IN REACHING THE FIRE

One or two firms of public adjusters keep automobiles waiting at certain "fixed posts" in the city, ready to carry their occupants to fires at a moment's notice. Usually, the first adjuster upon the scene succeeds in obtaining the contract. Adjusters cover all important fires, at all hours of the day or night.

Some adjusters—working in connection with brokers—make no effort to obtain signed contracts, but merely try to persuade the person having the loss to deal with the broker through whom the original policy was issued. As the adjuster always receives fifty per cent. of whatever adjusting business the broker recommends to him, this is only another and perhaps more dignified means of accomplishing the same object as obtaining signed contracts.

So many questionable things have been done by public adjusters in the arranging of claims, that the public is now becoming wary of the profession, and the assured welcomes any suggestion which frees him from the obligation of signing a contract. When an adjuster simply requests that the assured "refer the adjustment of the claim to the original broker through whom the insurance policy was obtained," it sounds like a very reasonable proposition. No contract is signed. But the assured does not know that the broker subsequently recommends the adjustment of the loss to the particular adjuster who "referred the assured to the broker," and that the broker and adjuster share their gains by a division of half-and-half.

All brokers obtain fifty per cent. of the fees of adjusters whom they recommend. Brokers and adjusters thus play into each other's hands; and the signing of a contract is avoided. The "warning" issued by the Board of Underwriters is of little avail in these cases.

Besides padding claims against insurance companies after fires, in order to obtain a larger percentage on the loss, adjusters frequently manage to appropriate to themselves a far larger share of the settlement than their legal ten per cent. Various devices are resorted to. Among others, the following scheme might be mentioned:

HOW THE ASSURED IS SWINDLED

A fire occurs in which a person sustains a loss which the company's own appraiser adjudges to be, say, $500. The public adjuster, who deals directly with the adjuster of the company—not permitting the assured to come in contact with the company or its agent in any way—informs the assured that "the best he could do" was $350, and is prepared to pay this amount. If the assured readily agrees to this sum, and appears to be ignorant and "easy," the adjuster pretends that "someone in the main office has to be fixed" and he gets the assured to agree to paying out further small sums; $5 to one party; $10 to another, and so on, until perhaps another $50 is deducted from the proffered $350. Finally, the assured receives perhaps $250, or less, out of a loss for which the company gave the adjuster a check for $500. Nobody is "any the wiser" in most instances, and where an adjuster is occasionally detected, the majority of persons having fire-losses are usually so ignorant that they accept the adjuster's statement without question.

Some companies refuse to pay losses through public adjusters, and insist upon dealing directly with the assured, handing the latter the check for the loss. In that case, the adjuster accompanies the assured to the office, a previous understanding having been arrived at to the effect that the 10 per cent. is to be paid over out of the check, and very often a further amount to "someone in the home office." Adjusters in these cases pretend that there is great difficulty in obtaining the check, and that company officials have to be "fixed" before the claim can go through. The secretary of one of the largest companies in America informed the writer that a certain adjuster had told the assured that he, the company's secretary, was looking for a hundred dollars out of a certain adjusted claim. The money was deducted from the check by the adjuster, who kindly cashed it for the assured. Needless to say, the amount supposedly set aside for "fixing" the company's secretary went directly to the pocket of the adjuster.

INCENDIARIES DEPEND ON ADJUSTERS

If such practices as these take place in the adjustment of legitimate claims, it stands to reason that adjusters play an equally questionable part in adjusting claims in fires of suspicious origin.

Incendiaries invariably employ adjusters to settle their claims after "made" fires. The dishonest broker and adjuster play a very important part in all fires of this character. In certain districts the fire bug and the insurance broker work hand in hand. Numbers of agents and adjusters solicit business among this class of people on the distinct understanding that fires will follow the issuance of policies. There is a fairly well authenticated story of an insurance agent working in a certain district of the city who, in delivering his fire insurance policies to his customers, always slipped a match under the rubber band around the policy. The suggestion was obvious.

Another broker, well skilled in the methods of the fire bug and his insurance "assistant" assured the writer that "very little business would be done by many brokers and insurance agents if it were only the commission on the policy which they were working for. It is the adjustment of the expected fire-loss that these agents want; and if fires do not result in a fair number of instances, business is considered very poor."

BROKERS, ADJUSTERS AND INSURANCE AGENTS, EITHER IN HAZARDOUS DISTRICTS OF THE CITY, OR IN SECTIONS WHERE CERTAIN CLASSES OF THE POPULATION ARE

KNOWN TO BE GIVEN TO INCENDIARISM, EXERCISE A DECIDED INFLUENCE ON THE TRADE OF "MAKING FIRES." WITHOUT THEIR TIMELY ASSISTANCE AND ADVICE, MANY FIRES OF INCENDIARY ORIGIN WOULD NOT TAKE PLACE; OR, IF THE FIRES OCCURRED, THE INSURANCE CLAIMS WOULD NOT BE PAID.

Some companies refuse to issue policies to applicants save through the agency of a broker. It is owing to this fact that many notorious fire bugs are able to obtain insurance policies even in districts of risky character. The brokers or agents in question frequently transact so large a business that the companies do not care to refuse any orders.

A tacit understanding exists to the effect that if a definite amount of first-class business is brought in, the broker or agent may also obtain certain policies without question. When fires occur in these last-mentioned cases the brokers obtain settlement of the claims with little difficulty, the payment of the loss promptly following the fire.

Apparently, it would not pay a company to insure parties who have fires and make claims; but all insurance companies depend upon the "law of averages." The immense volume of business done among, and the high premium paid by, reasonably honest people who never have fires bring in sufficient premium revenue to offset individual losses of the fire-bug fraternity.

Furthermore, increased premiums charged in areas where suspicious fires occur bring up revenues from the entire neighborhood sufficiently high to cover actual losses in individual cases.

Some companies actually boast of "prompt payment of losses," and even of the overpayment of claims. These companies are well known among the fire-making contingent of the population, and their names and methods of business are also known among their competitors. In substantiation of the statement as to the overpayment of losses, see letter from Mr. F. H. Ross on page 29 of this report.

COMPANY ADJUSTERS PAY CLAIMS TOO READILY

Out-of-town insurance companies largely depend upon certain of their own adjusters who, in the settlement of claims after fires, confer with adjusters appointed by the assured. Many of these adjusters—working for the companies—are unskilled in dealing with fires of suspicious character; especially those in which fire bug operatives have performed their work well. The company adjusters are frequently, under these circumstances, overreached by the more clever adjusters of the incendiaries, and recommend the payment of claims which a more experienced person—such as the Fire Marshal—would never sanction.

There is also another class of company adjuster that does not take the trouble to inquire too minutely into claims put forward by regular public adjusters. They are paid good salaries by their companies for adjusting claims, and if they can save a few hundred dollars or a few thousands on each claim, they consider their duties fully performed. Their main function consists, it appears, in driving a good bargain with the assured, or the adjuster representing him. Company adjusters of this character have been known to pay claims even when warned by officials of the Fire Department that the fires were probably of incendiary origin. Such methods on the part of these company adjusters cannot be too strongly condemned.

THE TOTAL LACK OF PROPER PREVIOUS INSPECTION OF

ALL PROPERTY TO BE INSURED, OR INQUIRY INTO THE CHARACTER OF THE PERSONS REQUIRING INSURANCE, IS MAINLY RESPONSIBLE FOR THE MAJOR PORTION OF INCENDIARY CRIMES. BROKERS AND AGENTS DO NOT HESITATE TO APPLY FOR THOUSANDS OF DOLLARS OF INSURANCE ON PROPERTY OF LITTLE OR NO VALUE, SIMPLY FOR THE SAKE OF OBTAINING THEIR COMMISSIONS. Many of these agents knowingly obtain policies on property which they are fully aware will be burned, expecting to receive not only the commission upon the policy, but also a large " rake-off " from the adjustment of the claim following the fire.

INSURANCE EXPERT ATTACKS ADJUSTERS

On the question of agents, brokers and adjusters, the words of a well-known insurance expert—Mr. Robert J. Lawrence, Insurance Statistician of the Spectator Company—might here be quoted:

> " Insurance agents," says Mr. Lawrence in a signed statement published January 25, 1912, " as a class are as honest as the average man who works on a commission basis. Unfortunately the financial interest of the agent is not identical with that of the company he represents. This conflict of interest is seen in every business done on a commission basis. *Many agents will insure a losing enterprise or the plant of a man whose dishonesty is notorious, or place an excessive valuation on a stock of goods or a building. To insure household furniture without knowledge of its real value is common.*
>
> " Seasons of financial panic or commercial depression," continues Mr. Lawrence, " aggregate the danger of loss to the fire insurance companies from incendiary fires. At such times, men who could not be justly charged with a willingness to set fire to their insured property, would not be annoyed by the discovery that the property had burned, provided it was insured.
>
> " Another phase of the moral hazard in fire insurance," says this writer, " is that which follows a perfectly straight fire-loss. A person whose property has been destroyed is approached *by a creature calling himself an independent fire insurance adjuster. This grafter proceeds to show the insured how easy it is to pad his claim* against the fire insurance company without any appreciable risk of discovery. Of course, he stipulates for a certain percentage of the overplus realized on the adjustment of the loss, and frequently men who are esteemed honest and upright succumb to the temptation so alluringly set forth by the unprincipled adjuster."

HOW TO REMEDY THE ADJUSTING EVIL

Rigid previous inspection of *all* proposed risks, diligent inquiry into the character of the assured, together with the placing of adjusters and brokers under bonds in addition to having them properly licensed, would do away with practically all " crooked " brokers and adjusters; and, at the same time, act advantageously upon the reduction of incendiarism.

Active co-operation among the Fire Department, Police Department, State Banking Department and State Insurance Department in the matter of granting licenses, and investigation of character of brokers and adjusters, would place this matter on its proper footing; and put an end to a condition which amounts to nothing more nor less than a public scandal at the present time.

CHAPTER VI.

Convictions for Arson in Five Years—The "Arson Trust"—Financial Conditions Directly Related to Incendiarism—The Fishman and Other Trials—Skill of Professional Fire Makers.

DURING the five years ending with December, 1911, in Greater New York 459 persons were arrested for the crime of arson. Of that number, 142 have been convicted. Magistrates have discharged, grand juries have failed to indict, or juries have acquitted 254 persons charged with arson. Persons of unsound mind and "Pyromaniacs" are not here included.

Judging from the small number of convictions, and the large percentage of persons against whom the charge of arson was brought, but not proven, the difficulties of conviction in such cases may be surmised. Only an intimate personal acquaintance with arson cases, and the almost superhuman efforts required to obtain convictions in such cases, will give the figures here mentioned proper significance.

Case after case is brought in our courts, and even where evidence seems overwhelmingly convincing, juries either fail to convict, grand juries fail to indict, or magistrates or judges discharge. In several cases where trials have taken place, juries have found parties "Not Guilty" in the face of evidence on which an unbiased person of sound judgment could not fail to bring in a conviction.

But, such is the nature of arson. And convictions in these cases seem growing even more difficult every day; yet not altogether from the failure of legal process.

The up-to-date fire bug is an entirely different personality from his fellow-craftsman of even ten years back. Where the early fire bug worked with kerosene, benzine, turpentine, or other common materials, the modern expert employs highly volatile substances of unusual composition, and evinces great skill and knowledge in the handling of chemicals and explosives, time fuses, and other devices. Complete and rapid destruction of property is brought about in a manner making it almost impossible of detection. By these methods evidence of incendiarism is wholly destroyed.

GREAT SKILL OF PROFESSIONAL INCENDIARIES

It is not proposed in this report to provide a Manual of "Fire Bug Methods" so that persons so inclined may learn how to operate, or what to avoid. Suffice it to say that the present-day operations of incendiaries are, as a rule, so skilfully performed that it is only by the merest "accident" —some failure of a well-laid plan—that Fire Marshals are able to bring any of these people to justice.

The stamping out of incendiarism by "catching fire bugs in the act" is almost impossible of attainment. Incessant vigilance on the part of present Fire Marshals has already acted as a decided deterrent in these cases; but

A GROUP OF CONVICTED FIRE BUGS

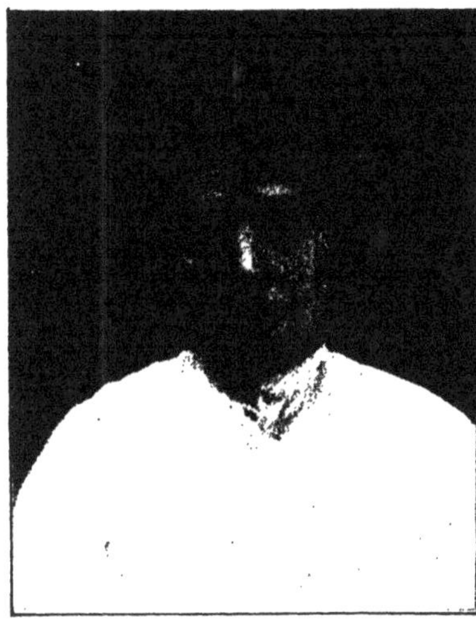

Mrs. Annie Singer
(See pages 95 to 99.)

Jacob Ostrinsky
(See pages 95 to 99.)

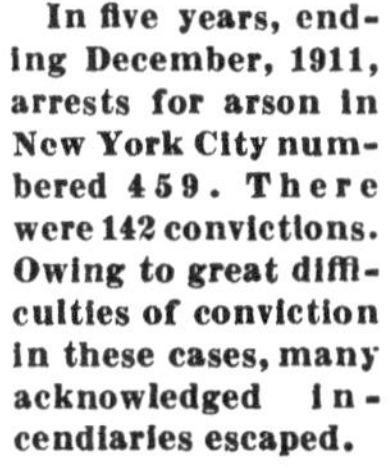

In five years, ending December, 1911, arrests for arson in New York City numbered 459. There were 142 convictions. Owing to great difficulties of conviction in these cases, many acknowledged incendiaries escaped.

Mrs. Annie Ackerley
(See pages 90 to 94.)

The convicted fire bugs shown on this page were engaged in the business of firemaking for insurance. By stopping the granting of policies to such people, Fire Insurance Companies can automatically end incendiarism.

Samuel Brant, "Fire Specialist"
(See pages 68 to 71.)

Benjamin Brownstein, Brant's Partner
(See pages 68 to 72.)

where incendiarism for gain is in the minds and systems, the very blood, of the people, as it seems to be to-day—where individuals and business firms look to fires in order to win easy money from insurance companies—THERE IS NO WAY OF PUTTING AN END TO THE EVIL BUT BY STOPPING THE ISSUANCE OF INSURANCE POLICIES UNDER THE PRESENT SYSTEM.

This is the only manner of reaching the root of the trouble.

While pointing out the real issue, however, and fixing responsibility where it actually belongs, a report of this description would be incomplete without acquainting the community with a few of the cases of incendiarism which, during recent years, have engaged the activities of Fire Departments in this and other cities.

Brief reference—before taking up New York cases—might be made to the operations of the Chicago gang, better known as the "Arson Syndicate," particularly in view of the fact that members of this gang from time to time visit New York, and are known to have worked in this district. The Chicago affair also throws much light on methods pursued in New York to-day.

Affidavits made in Chicago before Fire Attorney Michael Sullivan a year or two ago revealed the presence of a secret band of fire makers who might well be termed the "Arson Trust" in view of their extensive operations.

Working in connection with crooked insurance adjusters and insurance men, eager to pile up big records of business, it is estimated that these people destroyed upwards of $10,000,000 worth of property in eight years.

OPERATIONS OF THE "ARSON TRUST"

What first drew the attention of public authorities in Chicago to the presence of members of this gang was the remarkable evidence brought out in connection with the suicide in June, 1911, of Leopold Dreyfus, member of a firm of wholesale clothiers at 232 South Market Street, Chicago. Three days before his death, he had had a fire in his place, on which an insurance claim of $15,000 had been made.

Owing to the fact that this firm had had several previous fires of suspicious character, the public authorities decided to investigate. It developed, during the course of the inquiry that the Dreyfus Brothers had had "crooked" fires in the past; and upon Leopold Dreyfus being put under arrest, he confessed. His brother, a partner in the firm made the following statement:

> "We had known the principal agent of the arson crowd for some time. He is a man with six children and owns property in Chicago. About four months previous to this last fire he came to us and showed us how easy it would be to have a fire and collect insurance. This was at our Lincoln Avenue store. We made a deal with his associates and himself, and on February 15, the fire was carried out as planned. We collected the insurance without trouble.
>
> "Then we started a clothing factory on South Market Street. The agent of the fire bugs solicited the job of firing it for us. He was known as the 'solicitor,' because he went about obtaining orders for fires. Last week my brother made a contract with him to do the job for $2,000.
>
> "'Do you guarantee to make a clean job of it?' my brother asked.
>
> "'I take a risk, and you take a risk,' was the answer.

"The agent was paid $150 on Friday and $150 on Saturday just before the blaze. They were to have had $1,700 yesterday, but there was too much 'smoke' about the fire.

"The agent came up to the store early on Saturday. My brother went carefully out of town. Before noon an expressman delivered six five-gallon jugs of gasoline, bringing them up on the freight elevator. The fire bug agent was there to receive them. Then came the fire.

"My brother had another scheme for working the insurance game. He would induce other merchants to have fires in their store and make claims on goods which were never in the place. He would supply regularly receipted bills for the goods, and, of course, the insurance companies could not dispute them; and would have to pay."

HOW FIRE MAKERS OBTAIN "CUSTOMERS"

During the cross-examination of Leopold Dreyfus before the District Attorney it was revealed that the firm was on the verge of bankruptcy. They had liabilities of more than $32,000 with only $20,000 of assets. Besides this, there were heavy personal debts, which were very pressing.

It was just at this psychological moment that the "solicitor" of the fire bugs appeared upon the scene, and offered to burn out the Market Street store for $5,000; but Leopold Dreyfus said this sum was too high; and also refused to pay more than 10 per cent. of the insurance which he would collect.

In order to manufacture an alibi, Leopold Dreyfus on the day before the fire, went to Round Lake, Ill., and remained there until the fire occurred. His brother, Lazarus, remained in Chicago, but was not at the fire when it took place.

Owing to the suspicious character of the fire, and the fact of their former troubles in the same line, the insurance companies deferred paying the claims of the Dreyfus firm; and, finally the confession of Leopold Dreyfus was obtained. After making this confession, the fire bug merchant was permitted to go home with a detective. On reaching his home, he absented himself on some pretext or other; and during the short interval, managed to commit suicide. Detective Wulf, of the Chicago force, was completely nonplussed by the "escape" by death of his prisoner. The District Attorney was also greatly disappointed, as he expected to obtain from Dreyfus further statements leading to the discovery of many Chicago crooks, with bands of whom the latter had been long working.

Besides engaging in "fire bug" business, Leopold Dreyfus had also been involved in several transactions of a financial character which did not reflect credit upon him. Among other things, he had—shortly before the fire—discounted a number of his accounts, for which he received money from certain banks and collection agencies. These agencies found, however, that he had falsified many of the accounts and himself collected a number of the items. The accounts were returned to him, and prosecutions begun; but, of course, his death forestalled all these actions.

Fishman Loft After the Fire. Note Boxes and Oil Soaked Trailers.
(For particulars see pages 63 to 64.)

Fire Bug "Plant" Found at 89 Mercer Street, Manhattan, July 25, 1911. Large Box on Ground Filled with Inflammable Oil. Note Trailers Leading to Tables. **(See pages 63 to 64.)**

CLOSE RELATION BETWEEN ARSON AND LOW FINANCES

After the Dreyfus affair in Chicago, H. H. Glidden, General Manager of the Chicago Board of Underwriters, made the following statement:

> "*Arson as a regular business is being carried on in every large city in the world, but it is more common in this country than elsewhere.* Insurance men have been on the track of gangs of professional incendiaries for generations, and every now and then we have been able to get convicting evidence, send a bunch of fire bugs to prison and for a time break up the series of mysterious fires. But it seems impossible to put a stop to this sort of thing altogether."

Fire Attorney Sullivan, in commenting on the case, said the confession showed that *"solicitors" follow bankruptcy proceedings and give strict attention to the failures of small merchants. Women detectives aid in discovering financial conditions of merchants and report on the possibility of reaching a "prospect."* The object of the organization is to obtain insurance for the "customer" and *tide him over a financial crisis.* Spot cash "retainers" are demanded and usually 10 per cent. of the insurance is received.

THE FISHMAN CASE

Officials are not always able to discover fire bugs so easily as in the Chicago case, even though the material evidence of arson is equally convincing. For instance, there was a fire at 89 Mercer Street, New York, on the night of July 25, 1911, which bore all the evidence of incendiarism. The person tried was acquitted. The facts in this case are noteworthy as bearing on the difficulty of conviction in arson cases.

The fire happened about 11.45 o'clock, on a heavy, misty night; the atmospheric conditions doubtless having much to do with the subsequent discovery of evidence pointing to incendiarism.

A watchman engaged in taking care of premises on the opposite side of the street had observed smoke coming from the fourth floor of a loft building at the address mentioned. He sent in the alarm, and a quick response on the part of Batallion Chief Henry B. Helm, from Hook and Ladder No. 20, situated at 155 Mercer Street, disclosed the fact that the fire was caused by an ingenious fire bug "plant," consisting of ten or twelve pasteboard boxes—of the large kind suitable for packing clothing—which had been half-filled with inflammable oil.

The boxes were connected up with trailers of cloth, saturated with inflammable oil, which led through a wooden partition on the floor. In addition to the boxes soaked with combustible oil, a candle stuck through a piece of paper was discovered. Oil-saturated trailers and paper were distributed about the place.

Unfortunately for the plans of the incendiary, in addition to the general atmospheric conditions being unfavorable to the spreading of a blaze, certain circumstances within the loft structure had contributed to the failure of the "plant" owing to the fact that all air had been excluded by the closing and locking of the doors and windows. So anxious had been the incendiary that the fire would have a "good start" that he had placed heavy sheets of paper across the front windows, so that the blaze might not be prematurely seen from the street. By excluding all air, however, he had deprived the fire of necessary oxygen, and had thus defeated his own purpose.

So carefully had the building been locked up that firemen were compelled to enter from the outside front fire escape. They found every door and window securely fastened on the inside and the blaze smouldering in the oil-soaked boxes.

Chief Helm, on extinguishing the fire, immediately communicated with the Fire Marshal. The latter remained upon the scene most of the night, gathering evidence which plainly pointed to incendiarism.

THE EVIDENCE IN THE CASE

After due investigation, and careful consideration of all circumstances of the case, an indictment was found against the occupant of the loft, Morris Fishman.

It was brought out at the trial which took place before his Honor Judge James T. Malone, in the Court of General Sessions, that Fishman had, one month before the fire, increased his insurance from $2,500 to $7,500. Counsel for the State attempted to prove that the stock of goods on the premises never corresponded in value even to the smaller amount of insurance placed upon it; while the defendant's counsel maintained that Fishman frequently had on his premises goods belonging to customers of a value equal to the insurance carried.

The State was able to produce evidence showing that none had access to the premises but the defendant; and it was admitted by him that he had the only set of keys in his possession at the time of the fire. The partner of the defendant, one Dworkin, was absent from the city at the time.

At the time of the fire, the defendant was at home in a suburb of Brooklyn.

Fishman on his trial was ably defended. At the end of an exhaustive investigation, lasting from December 6 to December 15, the jury, after being out one hour and nineteen minutes, brought in a verdict of " Not Guilty."

At this fire, it was quite evident that arson had been committed by someone. Judge Malone instructed the jury that it was not necessary to find that the defendant himself had actually set the place on fire; but, if it could be shown that he was connected with anyone who had actually perpetrated the act, he would be equally culpable. While the State failed to fasten the guilt upon Fishman to the satisfaction of the jury, there was no doubt whatever that the crime of arson had been committed by someone, for there were the tell-tale boxes, the cloth trailers, for carrying the fire from one portion of the loft to another, the candle stuck through the paper, and the complete paraphernalia of the fire bug plant.

Had the night of the fire been a clear one, with a good wind, the fire at 89 Mercer Street—in the heart of the business district—might have spread throughout lower Manhattan. Had the private watchman who first discovered smoke issuing from the premises failed to occupy his exact post of observation at the critical moment, the consequences would have been serious, and all evidence of the plant might have been destroyed.

A CLEAR CASE OF ARSON BUT NO CONVICTION

Another case of undoubted arson, but in which the accused person was ordered by the Judge to be found " Not Guilty," was that of Biagio Calandra, a fruit merchant, occupying premises at 282 Washington Street, Manhattan. The fire occurred on the evening of March 18, 1908, at 7.05 o'clock, when a watchman saw smoke issuing from the first floor of the premises mentioned. The firemen on reaching the scene discovered a re-

Candle on Oil-Soaked Paper Found in Fishman Case.
(See pages 63 and 64.)

Box Filled with Oil, and Cloth Trailer (Oil-Soaked) Leading through Wooden Partition in Fishman Loft. (See pages 63 and 64.)

markable state of affairs: No less than 5 separate bladders, some containing turpentine, others ether, were suspended from barrels placed in the main aisle of the shop. The fire had started in the south-western corner of the building among some kegs of grapes and bags of nuts. Deputy Chief Guerin, now head of the Fire Prevention Bureau, was on the scene shortly after the fire started and pronounced it one of arson.

Oil soaked bagging and tissue paper fuses, in the form of trailers, led from bladders on barrels to adjacent parts of the store; and had not the Fire Department responded with the utmost promptitude, the whole place would have been completely destroyed. A bottle containing ether was also found.

THE REMARKABLE CALANDRA CASE

Calandra, the occupant of the first floor and basement, had left the premises about 5.15 P. M. on the day of the fire; the blaze having been discovered, as stated, shortly after 7 o'clock.

The total appraised value of the entire stock of goods in the Calandra place amounted to about $4,603.76. The insurance carried by him was $16,621.72.

Owing to the quick action of the Fire Department, the total damage was only $1,544.15.

An indictment was found against Calandra April 9, 1908.

At the trial, it appeared that Calandra had been supplied by a relative with various bills and invoices for fruit at $6 per barrel, which witnesses testified to as not being worth more than $2.50 per barrel. The large amount of over-insurance was also brought out in evidence. Furthermore, the defendant had made arrangements to lease another place, and to close up his then premises from the 1st of May—thirteen days prior to the occurrence of the fire.

As numbers of other persons had access to the Calandra premises besides the proprietor of the fruit shop, Judge O'Sullivan directed that he should be acquitted.

No doubt arson was committed by someone in this case. Despite all evidence of the bladders, trailers and oil-soaked bagging, no one was ever found guilty of this crime.

The Calandra fire was started in the heart of the great warehouse section, and had the Fire Department been slow in arriving upon the scene, a great fire, whereby New York may have lost millions of dollars, might have occurred.

The Calandra fire will always remain one of the unsolved mysteries of New York.

CHAPTER VII.

Incendiaries Caught "Red-Handed"—Gang of Horse-Burners Pour Gasoline on Animals and Attempt to Fire Stable—Gunpowder Plot Foiled by Fireman—Queer Circumstantial Evidence That Led to Conviction.

CATCHING fire bugs "in the act" may be considered among well-nigh impossible feats, and yet it has been done recently by Fire Marshals, both in the Boroughs of Manhattan and Brooklyn. One of the most interesting developments along this line was the operation of the Brooklyn Fire Marshal's Office in capturing Samuel Brant, a fire bug, now serving a long sentence in Sing Sing Prison, for setting fire to the premises No. 726 Cleveland Street, Brooklyn, N. Y., on the morning of December 18, 1911. In Manhattan, the rounding up of Isadore Steinkreutzer, an incendiary, with many fires to his credit, was also an important accomplishment. (For particulars, see pages 84 to 88.)

THE CASE OF SAMUEL BRANT

Brant had openly boasted of being a "specialist" in fire-making; that he could do his work so perfectly that no Fire Marshal would ever suspect him of the crime. With Morris Greenspan (recently convicted), aged 28, of 158 East 144th Street, The Bronx, and Benjamin Brownstein (also convicted), of 124 Second Street, Manhattan, Brant had arranged to set fire to the flat of Samuel Barr, at the Cleveland Street address.

The Brooklyn Fire Marshal, Mr. Thomas P. Brophy, ascertained, after trailing the fire bugs for some time, the hour at which the fire was to take place, and several members of his staff disguised themselves as street cleaners and peddlers and took up stations in front of the premises. In a push-cart beneath a load of potatoes and other vegetables were concealed a length of hose, some hand grenades and other fire fighting materials. The supposed peddlers and street cleaners consisted of Firemen John Nolan, Michael McCaffrey, John Kiernan, Henry Martin, Thomas Doran, Maurice Britt and James Mundy, chauffeur for Deputy Commissioner Farley.

Brant and Brownstein were playing the part of "boarders" in the Barr apartments, but as a matter of fact they had no status in the premises at all, being only there for the purpose of bringing off the fire. Despite the fact that Brant had no property in the premsies he had obtained insurance amounting to the sum of $500, the amount of insurance obtained by Barr being $800.

INCENDIARIES OBTAIN INSURANCE WITH EASE

No previous investigation was made by any of the companies prior to issuing this insurance to the fire bug, Brant, and to his partner Barr. Barr, a week or so prior to the date set for the fire, became conscience-stricken and made a clean breast of everything to Fire Marshal Brophy who thereafter used him for the purpose of obtaining evidence.

Just as the fire was about to take place, one of those curious incidents which often upsets "the best laid plans" happened: A policeman stationed himself very close to the premises, not knowing anything of the arrange-

A COLLECTION OF INCENDIARY MATERIALS

Various Fire Bug "Plants" now in Possession of the Brooklyn Fire Marshal. Several of these Consist of Bombs and Other Explosives. (See Galasso and other cases, Chapters VII. and VIII., pages 68 to 99.)

ments made by the Fire Marshal for effecting the capture of the fire makers "in the act." The Fire Marshal by writing a note and having it delivered by a woman occupying a nearby house, persuaded the officer to leave the spot for the time being. Shortly after the policeman absented himself, smoke was seen issuing from the windows of the Barr apartment and Brant and Greenspan came hurrying from the house. The Fire Marshal signalled for his supposed street sweepers and peddlers to close in, and himself confronted the fire bugs. One of them offered some resistance but was promptly knocked down; while the other was also quickly captured.

The fire in the house had made considerable headway, but with the length of hose and other apparatus in the pushcart it was soon extinguished.

Brant was tried before Judge Lewis L. Fawcett, in the County Court of Kings, Brooklyn, his trial lasting a whole week. He was convicted and sentenced to a term of 15 years.

A remarkable phase of the Brant case was the fact that the fire bug —without having any property at all in the premises—had secured $500 worth of insurance.

On the capture of Benjamin Brownstein at his furrier shop at 124 Second street, Borough of Manhattan, an insurance policy was found in his pocket showing that he had collected $100 on a fire at No. 83 Norfolk Street. This address was the one given as the home of Brant, proving that Brant and Brownstein were working together.

INCENDIARY BOASTS OF CRIME

Brant boasted to his confederates of having set fire to a number of houses and stated that he was in the regular fire bug business. A conversation was overheard by Abraham Flam, clerk in the Brooklyn Fire Marshal's Office, in which Brant praised himself as a "fire specialist," who had a method of producing fires in such a way that all evidence of incendiarism would be completely destroyed. Mr. Flam testified at the trial to having heard Brant say:

> "I am a specialist in making fires, and I can make them so they can't catch me. The Fire Marshal is a joke. If he gets you, all that you have to say is to tell him that you were away and get someone to prove it."

The three fire bugs worked a regular system. One of them would "solicit" business by going to the owner of a store, flat or small business concern, and offer to arrange for the insurance; at the same time planning the burning of the place. The three had other assistants, whose names have become known to the Fire Marshal.

The working of the Brant gang of fire bugs was on a similar order to that pursued by the Dreyfus crowd in Chicago, and the Paterson gangs. There is always a "solicitor" who discovers the insurance "prospect" and secures the insurance while the rest of the gang make the necessary arrangements for successfully bringing about the fire.

In the Brant case, the suspects were carefully trailed and "shadowed" for some days by various members of the Fire Marshal's office. One of them was hidden away in the premises, and actually overheard details of the plans for the proposed burning.

The features of the Brant case are typical of numbers of others. The fire started in a clothes closet. The presence of a "boarder" in these cases is characteristic. In most fires in the uptown district of Manhattan already described, the "boarder" is always in evidence, especially when it comes to filing claims against insurance companies.

Benjamin Brownstein was found guilty and convicted after a week's trial, ending September 16, 1912.

ATTEMPT TO BURN UP HORSES

One of the most dastardly events in the entire history of incendiarism was the attempt to burn seven decrepit horses in a stable in the rear of 363 Johnson Avenue, Brooklyn, on the night of August 14, 1912. The plot was frustrated and the band of firebugs captured. The leader of this band was Morris Greenberg, alias " The Torch," aged 65 years.

These fiends pursued an atrocious form of fire insurance swindle. It was their plan to insure good horses, and then substitute for them broken down hacks which they burned in order to collect insurance.

Fortunately for the poor horses in the case (see photograph on opposite page of this report), word had reached Fire Marshal Brophy of Brooklyn that an attempt would be made to set fire to the stable on a certain night. As they arranged their plans, the Fire Marshal in turn perfected his. For several days prior to the proposed attempt, the man owning the horses, the fire bugs, and other persons connected with the affair were assiduously shadowed. The owner of the horses, one Louis Evans, or " Evansky," of No. 215 Varet Street, in the Williamsburg District, had been attending auction sales in East New York and elsewhere, buying up numbers of decrepit and useless horses, some of which were lame and absolutely unfitted for work, to be substituted for the good horses in his stable.

On the horses installed by Evans at 363 Johnson Avenue—a deserted section of the Borough of Brooklyn—he obtained no less than $1,400 worth of insurance in the Northern Assurance Company of London. The agent who obtained the policies for Evans, Jacob Zamzok, of 69 Woodbine Street, Brooklyn, stated under oath that he had not inspected the horses at all before applying for the insurance. Nevertheless, the company had issued $1,400 worth of insurance on horses which were subsequently sold by Evans's wife, at least six of them, for the sum of $25, or $4.16 each. Had the " plugs " been burned up, claims for the 7 horses would have been made against the insurance company for $200 each, and receipted bills would doubtless have been produced, showing the values of the better horses for which they had been substituted.

The principal fire bugs in this affair were Morris Greenberg, aged 65, of 345 Blake Avenue, Brownsville; his son, David Greenberg, age 23, of the same address; Louis Evans, or " Evansky," truckman, of the address already mentioned, and Hyman Wasserman, a contractor, of 404 Blake Avenue. The Greenbergs, Evans and Wasserman admitted their guilt, the last named turning State's evidence, and making sensational disclosures.

MAGISTRATE'S SEVERE CENSURE

Magistrate Dodd, of the Manhattan Court, Brooklyn, held the prisoners without bail on a charge of arson, and remarked on reading the complaint:

> " The allegations in the complaint before me are so horrible that I could not for a moment consider such an application (for bail). I will send the prisoners to jail without bail, and I hope the District Attorney's office will be represented when the matter comes up for examination."

For a week prior to the night of the fire, the suspects had been trailed and a number of persons were employed on the case. Among others, were Miss Laura Grant, Inspector in the Bureau of Fire Prevention; Assistant

In Front Row: **Group of Self-confessed, Horse-Burning Fire Bugs. Captured at Stable, 363 Johnson Avenue, Brooklyn. Reading from Left to Right: David Greenberg, Morris Greenberg (centre), the Leader, Alias "The Torch," and Louis Evans, or Evansky.** *In the Rear are* **Their Captors—Members of the Staff and Assistants of the Brooklyn Fire Marshal.** **(For full particulars see pages 72 to 75.)**

Old Horse, Lame and Blind, Rescued by Fire Marshal Brophy and his Men on the Night of August 15, 1912. Held by First Grade Fireman John Nolan, who assisted in Capture of Fire Bugs. **(See pages 72 and 75.)**

Fire Marshals William R. Ferris, Eugene Shields, Gustav Werner, John Lyman, Richard Walsh and Israel Spielberg; Police Detective George Drum, of the Stagg Street Station; Clerk Flamm, of the Fire Marshal's Office, First Grade Firemen John Nolan, Michael McCaffrey and James J. Jones, No. 1, assigned to the Fire Marshal's Office, First Grade Fireman Joseph Fox, Deputy Chief O'Hara's chauffeur, and officers Schumann and Reichenbach of the Fire Patrol.

At last came the night appointed for the fire. The elder Greenberg and his son were trailed to the stable, Miss Grant and Assistant Fire Marshal Shields traveling with them part of the way from Brownsville on car No. 3954 of the Hamburg Avenue Line. Fire Marshal Brophy had surrounded the stable, placing armed assistants in the tall grass nearby, and on the tracks of the Long Island Railroad, which run behind the stable.

Captain Conway, of Engine 137, about three blocks away from the stable, had his engine hitched up in readiness for a prearranged signal of three shots from the Fire Marshal's revolver.

MIDNIGHT VIGIL AND SENSATIONAL CAPTURE

Shortly after midnight the watchers saw a glare of fire inside the stable and immediately afterwards the elder Greenberg and his son were seen coming from the rear of the stable, making their way through a hole under the mangers.

A whistle was blown; three shots were fired; the firemen in readiness started with their apparatus from the quarters of Engine Co. 137.

While the firebugs were struggling with their captors, other attaches of the Fire Department had gone to the rescue of the horses and were combating the fire.

When an entrance into the stable was effected one of the most dastardly plants ever devised by a human being was discovered. There were three fires burning within the stable. One inside the doorway, a second a few feet away, and another in a corner immediately behind the seven helpless horses which were haltered to the mangers. The coats of two horses were saturated with kerosene and gasolene. One of these animals was blind. Another was lame.

The fire burning inside the doorway of the stable was so arranged by these fiends as to block the only access in case of possible rescue, and did indeed for a time hinder and make more dangerous the work of the men who foiled the plot.

Great personal danger attended all those immediately engaged in this capture, owing to the notoriously desperate character of the elder Greenberg, and also to the fact that he had intended using explosives in making the fire.

FIRE BUG MAKES CONFESSION

Evans (whose real name is said to be "Evansky"—a native of Warsaw, Polish Russia), owner of the horses, confessed on the night of his capture that he had hired the two Greenbergs to set the stable on fire. He had promised them $100 for the job.

These horse-burning fiends were arraigned before Judge Norman J. Dike, in the County Court, Brooklyn, on December 16, 1912, and sentenced to prison terms as follows: Morris Greenberg, 10½ to 20½ years; David Greenberg, his son, 5½ to 10½ years; and Louis Evans, or Evansky, 7½ to 14½ years—all in Sing Sing Prison.

A similar case occurred in Manhattan on July 30, 1903. A fire bug plant was found in a stable at 210-214 Cherry Street, near Canal. The "plant" was found burning at 12.44 A. M. In the stable at the time were upwards of sixty horses, which would have perished miserably had not smoke attracted attention and resulted in calling the Fire Department in time. Six separate and distinct fires had been started in stalls of the stable, the plants consisting of candles set in among straw, which had been saturated with kerosene oil. Trailers led from the plants to different places about the stable.

For this fire Joseph Greenfeder, aged 20 years, was indicted August 28, 1903, but the indictment was dismissed by Judge Newburger, owing to the fact that it could not be proved that the man indicted for the crime had "exclusive access" to the stable. Owing to the dismissal of the indictment against Joseph, his brother, Isaac, was also released. A large amount of insurance had been placed upon the contents of the stable by the Greenfeders.

LARGE NUMBER OF SUSPICIOUS STABLE FIRES

Unfortunately, there are many cases of stable fires on record, and numbers of them are of suspicious origin.

It would seem that human depravity could descend to no lower depths than to burn living horses. The large number of stable fires, however, the cause of which is marked "Not Ascertained," leads to the conclusion that a considerable number of these fires are of suspicious origin. Out of 68 stable fires in the Boroughs of Manhattan, Bronx and Richmond reported for the year 1911, 22—nearly 33 per cent.—were of unknown origin.

However much sympathy might be lavished on dumb animals burned to death by the machinations of these soulless fire-fiends, it must not be lost sight of that they are also engaged in causing numerous "Tenement House" fires. Large numbers of these fires are of mysterious origin. Most cellar fires in tenements are of incendiary character. The question of loss of life does not seem to occur to the mind of the incendiary. His one thought is to obtain the money from his insurance policy.

Even where fires do not occur in tenements, *every* incendiary fire *may* result in loss of life.

Catching a fire bug "in the act," naturally, operates as a decided deterrent to the commission of crimes of this character by other incendiaries, especially where the captures are followed by effective handling of the cases when brought to trial. The pursuit of this work is often attended by great danger to those engaged in it.

FIREMAN PREVENTS DANGEROUS EXPLOSION

A case in which the elements of danger were strongly emphasized was that of Andrea Galasso, 4101 Eighth Avenue, Brooklyn, corner of 41st Street. The incident happened on the night of July 31, 1910, at 9.20 o'clock.

Galasso, an Italian, aged 46, with a family of five children, was convicted of having fired his two-story frame building. The first floor was occupied as a store, with a kitchen in the rear; the second being used as a grocery and shoe store.

Discovery of the fire in Galasso's place was accidental: Fireman James Halpin—who afterwards received a gold medal for his brave conduct in extinguishing this dangerous fire—had just come home, on leave of absence from Engine Company 18, in West 10th Street, Manhattan. His

Stable and Decrepit Horse—Bought by Louis Evans or Evansky Three Days Before the Fire for $6—which Fire Bugs Morris Greenberg and His Son David Attempted to Burn at Midnight on August 15, 1912. (See Chapter VII., pages 72-75.)

Interior of Stable Showing "Plant" to Burn Horses. Note Large Quantity of Paper, also Bottle of Gasolene. Horse's Leg Shown to Left. (Chapter VII., pages 72-75, etc.)

Hole under Manger from which Horse-burning Fire Bugs Morris and David Greenberg Emerged after Setting Fire to Stable. **(See Chapter VII., pages 72 and 75.)**

home was a short distance from the Galasso place in Brooklyn. Just as he was entering his doorway he saw in Galasso's basement what looked like a gleam of fire. Some people were running in the direction of the store.

Fireman Halpin ran to the Galasso home, and, smashing in a rear door, which led into a hallway, entered the kitchen. There was a strong odor of illuminating gas; and a lounge was on fire. He shoved the lounge through the rear window into the yard. As he did so, he noticed something burning on the floor, and put his foot on it.

The Fireman managed to get a light. He also cut off the gas. Halpin then found that he had put his foot on a portion of a candle, attached to a fuse connected with a large bomb containing several pounds of giant powder —sufficient, had it exploded, to have blown him to atoms.

Halpin was about to rush out to call the Fire Marshal—thinking the fire entirely extinguished—when a bystander informed him that there appeared to be another fire upstairs. At the risk of his life he rushed upstairs and found a bed on fire. He saw a sputtering in the mattress, and throwing a chair through the window to afford an opening, tossed the mattress out. He found a candle burning brightly on a lounge and extinguished it. The lounge was saturated with kerosene oil.

LARGE QUANTITY OF GIANT POWDER FOUND

On another bed was a newspaper, placed in the mattress, and inside the newspaper a large quantity of gun-powder. This giant-powder was also connected with a fuse, which was burning. Halpin put it out.

In fact, Fireman Halpin, single-handed and alone, put out this fire; and then notified the Fire Marshal and called a policeman to take charge, instructing him not to let anyone disturb the place.

Galasso, when arrested, had in his possession his fire insurance policies—calling for an amount greatly in excess of the value of his property. On his person were also found his marriage certificate, a deed to some property, baptismal papers of his children, and most of his valuable papers.

He denied all knowledge of the conditions and explained that he had been visiting relatives on Staten Island.

He had left his children at the home of a relative in Brooklyn on the day of the fire. He denied having any knowledge of explosives; though it was subsequently ascertained by Fire Marshal Brophy that Galasso had served his time in the Italian Army.

The trial of Galasso proved an interesting one. It took place before Judge Norman J. Dike. The defendant's strong point was his alibi; but the prosecution was able to prove that the fire had been carefully timed; that the defendant was greatly over-insured; and that he was, at the time of the fire, in financial difficulties.

Where there is alleged incendiarism, it is essential in law to connect the defendant either by direct evidence, or by a chain of circumstances sufficient to show that he was guilty beyond doubt. In this case, it was further proved that the place was locked; that defendant was the last person in the building; and that the "plants" were so arranged that the fire would not take place before defendant had a good chance to manufacture his alibi.

Judge Dike sentenced Galasso to five years in Sing Sing.

CONVICTED BY CIRCUMSTANTIAL EVIDENCE

As showing the curious nature of evidence on which convictions in arson trials are occasionally obtained, the case of Isadore Tirnauer might be cited. He was convicted on May 15, 1912, and sentenced on May 31, 1912, the trial taking place before Judge Bart J. Humphreys, in the Queens County Court. Tirnauer was found guilty of arson in the second degree, and sent to prison for a term of not less than five and not more than ten years. Tirnauer is a Russian Jew, age 28, with a wife and two children.

This man had had a previous fire at 118 Rockaway Road, Jamaica, Borough of Queens, on April 11, 1911; and, on that occasion the Brooklyn Fire Marshal had suspected him, but, not being able to obtain the evidence, he had given Tirnauer a warning. From that date, the Fire Marshal had kept him under observation, expecting another fire, as he had successfully collected from the Jamaica fire $600 insurance.

On the morning of March 21, 1911, the second Tirnauer fire came. It took place in a candy and stationery store at 2604 Jamaica Avenue, Richmond Hill.

A singular train of circumstantial evidence finally landed Tirnauer behind the bars.

On the morning of the date mentioned, at 5.40 o'clock, Policeman Charles M. Smith, of the 283d Precinct, was on patrol in the neighborhood of Tirnauer's store, and saw a man with a bundle of newspapers going down a side street about 5.30 o'clock. He watched this man, and saw him throw away a metal article, which the policeman picked up.

It proved to be a portion of a toy cash-register, made of black enamelled metal.

Policeman Smith walked towards Jamaica Avenue, and came upon the store, which was on fire. It had been discovered by Motorman Charles Miller, who was passing in his car. There was a decided odor of kerosene oil about the place, which was locked.

An alarm was turned in and while they were waiting for the fire apparatus, who should come upon the scene but the same man whom Policeman Smith had seen carrying the bundle of papers down the side street, and who had thrown away the metal register!

INDICATIONS OF A SUSPICIOUS FIRE

The store was completely gutted. The Fire Marshal considered the fire of suspicious character owing to the fact that the fire had jumped clear across the sidewalk, and set fire to a telegraph pole some ten feet away.

Fire Marshal Brophy confronted the owner of the store—Tirnauer—and asked the latter if he remembered having been warned about the previous fire at the Rockaway address. Tirnauer denied ever having seen the Fire Marshal before; and also disclaimed any knowledge of the cause of the present blaze. He finally admitted having collected $600 of insurance on the previous fire.

Aided by Assistant Fire Marshals William Ferris and William Anderson, the Brooklyn Fire Marshal now began a systematic study of the conditions. It was several months before Tirnauer was arrested, and during that time he was kept under close observation.

The difficulty in the case was that all evidence had been totally destroyed. The fact that the fire had eaten into the boards more deeply at one particular spot—where the oil had been—and that it had leaped across the pavement were the only tangible indications of incendiarism.

The defendant claimed that he had had about $1,000 worth of stock in the place, but investigation disclosed that he had a number of creditors, and not more than $200 worth of stock at the outside.

Hidden Dangers of "Fire Bug Plant." Giant Powder Bomb Found by Fireman Halpin in Brooklyn House. Every Gas Jet in Room was Turned on. Fireman Stepped on Candle Attached to Blasting Fuse Connected to Large Quantity of Gunpowder in Oil-Saturated Papers. Excelsior in Mattress in Crib Oil-soaked and Exposed to Flames. (See Galasso case, pages 76-79.)

BALANCE IN BANK ONLY SIX CENTS

His bank account in the Hillside Bank was the sum of exactly 6 cents. Some checks were discovered as having been returned marked "Insufficient funds."

Tirnauer shortly before the fire had borrowed money.

In a carefully prepared statement he gave an account of his whereabouts on the morning of the fire. He said he had arrived at his store about 5.30 o'clock and had found a bundle of newspapers, with a penny on the top, which a customer had left. He had unlocked the door and turned up the gas by means of a string, which he only had to pull. He had used no matches. He was there but a short time, and had turned the light down and walked out, locking the door.

When shown the portion of the cash register which the policemen had seen him throw away, he declared that he had never seen it before.

On searching the remains of this fire a burned cash register was found similar to the one Tirnauer had thrown away, and he was told of this. He admitted that he had had several cash registers of that kind in his store for sale, but denied that any significance could be attached to the piece of one which the policeman had found.

TOY CASH REGISTER LEADS TO CONVICTION

Tirnauer parried every point with suavity and skill. He admitted that his wife had kept $2 in a toy cash register in the store. The whole case seemed to hinge upon this little toy cash register. It furnished a unique point of circumstantial evidence. The prosecution produced the partly burned one found in the store, and the portion of the one found by Policeman Smith, as "exhibits" of great importance in the case.

Counsel for the defence also had a brand new toy cash register in court and displayed a circular reading:

> "To open the Bank, place $10 in coin. It will then open automatically. If you don't deposit $10 in coin, you will have to get an axe."

Much stress was laid on the impossibility of opening the bank without an axe. It was expected by this to prove that Tirnauer could not have opened the box with his fingers on the street, in the manner described by Policeman Smith.

When the jury had retired they sent for the little cash register belonging to the defence. One of the jurors, by means of a pen-knife, opened the box in less than three minutes.

Result: Conviction and sentence to not less than five years in Sing Sing.

Tirnauer carried $700 insurance on his stock in the Fire Association of Philadelphia.

A significant point about this insurance is the fact that *though he had had a previous suspicious fire on which he had collected $600 he had experienced no difficulty in providing himself with further insurance.*

It was somewhat difficult at first to find a motive for Tirnauer's conduct, but it developed during the course of the investigation prior to his arrest that he had been trying to dispose of his business and that he was financially embarrassed. Had the insurance companies made any inquiry into his financial standing—quite irrespective of his previous fires—it is doubtful if they would have granted him the policy.

CHAPTER VIII.

Capture of a Famous Manhattan Fire Bug—Isadore Steinkreutzer and His Many Alibis—Closet Fires His Specialty—Some Famous FEMALE FIRE BUGS and Their Mode of Operation—Brief Outline of Recent Prosecutions.

AN extremely important capture and conviction in Manhattan recently was that of the man responsible for numerous fires in the district described as the "Fire Bug Zone." This was Isadore Steinkreutzer, 26 years old, of 114 East 97th Street. Steinkreutzer is known under several aliases, such as "Izzy Stein," "Kid Twist" (adopted after the demise of the gun-man killed at Coney Island a year or two ago), Izzy "the Paintner" (Painter in Russian), Isaac Chernick, Izzie Cohen, Izzie Gruber, and "Itchia der Warcher." He is said to have caused 300 fires.

For some months previous to the seizure of the man with the many aliases, he had been shadowed and followed by members of Fire Marshal John P. Prial's staff in Manhattan, and his operations had also been known to Chief William Guerin, head of the Fire Prevention Bureau, and to Battalion Chief John Howe, also of the Bureau. These two had taken an active part in keeping him under observation.

TIME OF OCCURRENCE IN INCENDIARY FIRES

Most fires brought about by the convicted fire bug were started in clothes-closets, a species of fire the origin of which, as already stated, is most difficult to determine. A somewhat remarkable feature of these fires is the fact that they almost always occurred between 10 A. M. and 3 P. M., the most opportune hours for occupants of apartments wishing to profit by fires to be absent from home and to prove convenient alibis. Few persons in this neighborhood who desire fires, make them themselves. The actual fire-making is done by professionals, or "fire specialists," such as Brant, Steinkreutzer and others.

On June 11, 1912, intimation was conveyed through a confidential source to Fire Marshal Prial and also to Chiefs Guerin and Howe that a certain Samuel Gold and his wife, living at 63 East 118th Street, and occupying the fifth floor front apartment, intended to employ the services of Steinkreutzer for the purpose of having a fire on June 19. Previous to the time mentioned, fire insurance to the extent of $1,200 had been secured on the Gold flat.

INCENDIARY FIRE STOPPED BY FUNERAL

It was subsequently ascertained by Fire Marshal Prial that the fire proposed for June 19 had been postponed for a few days, owing to the fact

"Plant" in Clothes Closet. Note Oil-Soaked Trailers Leading up into Closet. Also Matches on Floor. Clothes Closet Fires were Steinkreutzer's "Specialty." (Pages 84-88.)

"Fire Bug Plant" Showing Newspapers Pinned to Drawers and Oil-Soaked Material in Box with Candle.

that a funeral would take place from the adjoining house on the day set for the fire. Fire bugs, it seems, have qualms of conscience when it comes to burning up dead people!

On the morning arranged for the fire, after the difficulties caused by the awkward funeral had been overcome, Steinkreutzer and Gold were "shadowed" by various members of Fire Marshal Prial's staff. The two alleged incendiaries were seen at 6.30 A. M. to enter a saloon on Second Avenue near 102d Street, remaining in this place for an hour and a half.

Gold, on coming out, went to his tailor shop in Brooklyn, 517 Ninth Street, while Steinkreutzer made preparations for the fire. While going about this work he was watched at various times by Fire Marshal Prial, Assistant Fire Marshals de Malignon, Wade, Croker, Sheehan, Dilman, and First Grade Fireman Howe. All these persons were disguised as "tramps." Even the trained eye of Steinkreutzer failed to notice anything suspicious in the sudden surplus of loafing, ill-clad people in the immediate vicinity of his operations in the Gold apartment in East 118th Street.

At 10 o'clock Mrs. Gold was seen to leave the flat. A few minutes after her departure Fireman Howe and Assistant Fire Marshal de Malignon saw Steinkreutzer enter the building in which was located the Gold flat.

As Steinkreutzer entered the building, Assistant Fire Marshal Wade took a stand close to the fire-alarm box, corner of Madison Avenue and 118th Street. He awaited a signal from the watchers within the building announcing that the fire was under way.

RESPONSIBILITY OF FIRE MARSHALS

The anxiety and responsibility of Fire Marshals in these emergencies is little understood by the public. With them rests the onus of immediately extinguishing the fire which they have—after a fashion, and for the purpose of obtaining evidence—permitted to be started. If Fire Marshals prevented incendiaries whom they were watching from actually starting the blaze, there would be no evidence and no possibility of ever making a "red-handed" capture.

At the same time, an enormous weight of responsibility rests on the shoulders of Fire Marshals, for, if fires so started should get beyond control and destroy property or result in loss of life, blame for such loss—owing to their previous knowledge of the event—might seem to rest on them. Even after the fire is started and firemen are on the scene, it is possible that fire bug "plants" may result in serious explosions—such as the Paterson and Galasso cases—which might kill firemen and others immediately engaged in the dangerous work.

Furthermore, a criminal prepared to set fire to a building and to destroy property and burn up human beings, thinks little of using every means to defend himself; and to attack when cornered. All persons engaged in capturing fire bugs "in the act" run imminent risk of being killed or injured, either by the incendiary himself or by his fires.

As soon as Fireman Howe and Assistant Marshal de Malignon ascertained that Steinkreutzer had entered the Gold apartment they secreted themselves on the landing above, and a few minutes after saw him come out of the apartment and close the door behind him. He then went rapidly downstairs. The watchers pressed against the rear door of the apartment, and smelled smoke. They immediately signalled Assistant Fire Marshal Wade to turn in the alarm.

Howe then went through an adjoining apartment to the fire-escape and forced the windows of the Gold rooms. The door was forced by de Malignon. They found a fire burning in a clothes closet. The place was saturated with gasolene. The fire was quickly extinguished.

SMOKES CIGARETTE WHILE WATCHING BLAZE

Steinkreutzer, in the meantime, was seen to take up a point of observation on a fire-escape on the opposite side of the street, and was calmly smoking a cigarette and awaiting the arrival of the fire engines. He did not know, of course, that the alarm had been sent in, but was waiting to see the flames burst from the building, and doubtless hoped to enjoy the excitement of the discovery of the fire which he made.

Steinkreutzer after the arrival of the apparatus hastened to his home in East 97th Street and removed his coat. With remarkable coolness he then quietly strolled out and went into a saloon in 97th Street.

It was while he stood in this place, chatting with some friends—and apparently unconscious of anything in the nature of a fire having been started at 63 East 118th Street—that Assistant Fire Marshal Wade captured him at the point of a revolver, the first arrest, by the way, performed by any of the Fire Prevention Bureau force in their capacity as peace officers.

In the Gold apartment was found an insurance policy in Isadore Steinkreutzer's name, on the contents of an apartment formerly occupied by him at 549 Bushwick Avenue, Brooklyn. He had had a fire at that address.

Samuel Gold and his wife were arrested.

Among other published statements concerning the operations of Steinkreutzer is one that he is the alleged leader of a number of bands of fire bugs, working not only in Manhattan, but in Brooklyn, Queens and outlying points. A connection is said to exist between these various fire bug bands in the city, for fires in different sections display the handiwork of similar operatives; and the methods pursued by one fire bug are most characteristic. Some fire bugs, such as Steinkreutzer, confine themselves to fires in clothes closets; others use " quick flash " fires which blow out apartments and rapidly destroy all evidence of incendiarism. A skilled examiner into incendiary methods can readily discriminate between various pieces of work done by the same fire bug; just as the detective recognizes at a glance the workmanship of the expert safe-blower.

Steinkreutzer was tried and convicted before Judge Jos. F. Mulqueen, sitting in General Sessions, Manhattan, on November 22, 1912. He was sentenced November 27, 1912, to not less than twelve years or more than twenty-four and one-half years in State prison.

MONTHS OF PATIENT WORK TO TRAIL INCENDIARIES

The difficulties in the way of trailing these criminals are extremely great. It takes painstaking work, combined with the utmost patience, in order to obtain a line upon their operations. Crimes of incendiarism are planned, as a rule, months ahead and every detail is worked out to the last analysis before an attempt is made to " do the job."

Many times, in the trailing of fire bugs, actual fires are started by them almost under the eyes of observers; and yet there is not sufficient evidence at the time to cause an arrest. Where fire bugs can be seized in the very act of placing the match or applying the torch the conditions for bringing the charge home are ideal. However, such chances as these rarely occur;

and as a rule, are often the result of certain extraneous "accidents," such as the failure of incendiary plans, or similar events—which thus open up the channels of information leading to successful capture.

FIRE-MAKERS WELL ORGANIZED IN DIFFERENT CITIES

Fire bugs do not confine themselves to their own cities; but operate over a wide area. Boston, Chicago, and Paterson fire bugs not infrequently visit New York for the purpose of carrying out their plans. This method helps to baffle the police and Fire Marshals in the different cities.

Paterson, N. J., for instance, has a very enterprising and well organized band of incendiaries, who have many affiliations in New York City.

The operations of the Paterson fire bug organization were shown by the remarkable fire that occurred at the shop of Mathew, or Max, Pearlman, 25 Godwin Street, Paterson, at 10.30 A. M. June 19, 1912.

At the time mentioned a terrific explosion shook the small frame building at this address. The little shop of Max Pearlman, which occupied the ground floor, was totally wrecked. Flames burst from the front and rear windows. A family named Simmonds, living on the top floor of the ramshackle, three-story frame structure, had difficulty in making their escape. The children were carried down through the smoke by means of a ladder in the rear.

Firemen, arriving on the scene after the fire, discovered the body of an unknown man in the kitchen in the rear of the first floor. He was burned beyond recognition and died in the hospital immediately on arrival.

Concurrent with the explosion a man was seen to leap from a window of the building. His face and hands were severely burned. He made his escape over a fence and outhouse, but not before a good view of him had been obtained by several people.

OFFERED TO MAKE FIRES FOR $25 DOWN

A few weeks prior to this explosion in Godwin Street, Paterson, two men had gone about in the neighborhood where the fire occurred and "solicited" the job of setting fire to nearby property for the purpose of obtaining insurance. They offered to burn out one man's place for $25 down "on account" and a share of the subsequent insurance proceeds. Their offer was rejected. Shortly after this the fire occurred in the Pearlman place.

Mrs. Pearlman, just before 10.30 o'clock on the morning in question, had locked up her store and taken her child to Dr. Morris Joelson for the alleged purpose of having the child vaccinated. She claims to know nothing of the fire or of the dead man found in her place.

In the building where the explosion occurred various sums of insurance had been taken out, amounting altogether to $9,750, *though the property was estimated as not worth more than* $2,500. *The Pearlmans had recently insured their belongings to the extent of* $1,200.

Pearlman was away in New York at the time of the fire; Mrs. Pearlman also, as stated, was not on the scene.

FIRE MAKER HOIST BY HIS OWN PETARD

The body of the man killed by the explosion was subsequently identified as that of Jacob Horowitz, of 104 East 4th Street, Manhattan. Mrs. Horowitz, who went to Paterson to assist in the identification, stated that she was glad her husband was dead. "*For three years,*" she said, "I have been expecting something like this to happen. Now, I am glad. Glad for the children and for myself. They will not have to be like him," said this woman. This statement shows that a dangerous fire bug had been "operating" in New York for three years.

The man who escaped from the Paterson fire, whose name and record as a notorious and dangerous incendiary are known, was recently arrested in Brownsville, Brooklyn, and positively identified by two people from Paterson. Though recognized by these persons from Paterson as the man seen jumping over the fence after the explosion in the Pearlman place, he was allowed to go free by the New York authorities, owing to a trivial mistake in the spelling of his name in the New Jersey extradition papers. No effort was made to hold him under arrest until the error could be rectified; and he is now again free to prey upon the community. He is disfigured by burns from the Paterson explosion and his right thumb is missing.

WOMEN EXPERT IN MAKING FIRES

SOME FAMOUS FEMALE FIRE BUGS

Annie Ackerly;
Mattie Michaels;
Mrs. Annie Singer;
and others.

"Female fire bugs" play an important part in incendiarism. Many an innocent looking "curtain and gas jet" blaze, kerosene or benzine flare-up, or clothes-closet fire is the skilfully executed work of the woman incendiary.

In the "Fire Bug Profession" men by no means exercise a monopoly. Some of the most adroit fire-operatives are women. Strangely enough, in the congested districts of the city, among portions of the population addicted to the habit of having fires, elderly women and mothers of families do not hesitate to "make fires" whenever suitable opportunity arises. Cases have come to the attention of Fire Marshal Prial where grandmothers in certain families have applied the torch of arson; particularly in those most difficult of incendiary cases—clothes-closet fires.

ANNIE ACKERLY, THE "FEMALE FIRE BUG"

A woman fire bug case which attracted much attention a few years ago was the Annie Ackerly affair in Brooklyn. The fire occurred at 114 Wyckoff Street on December 10, 1907.

It was in an apartment house. Other families besides this woman occupied the premises, and, had her plans succeeded, several lives would have been lost.

Sleeping in the apartment below the Ackerly woman was a family with little children who were awakened by hot water dripping down upon them from the flat above. On investigation, a fire was found blazing in the Ackerly woman's apartments, the heat having melted the water pipes, water from which had dripped down through the ceiling. Had it not been for this fortunate accident other tenants in the house might have been burned to death.

The occupant of the apartment in which the fire occurred was absent. She had taken her three children and gone to Port Jefferson, Long Island. Incendiaries invariably absent themselves and are thus able to provide an alibi when the proper time comes. She was traced by a clue found in a letter.

After the Fire Department had succeeded in putting out the fire a remarkable state of affairs was disclosed. Several "time plants" were found in

"Plant" in Drawer of Chiffonier—Annie Ackerley Case (pages 90 to 94.) Note Candle in Midst of Kindling Wood in Drawer.

sideboards, cupboards and closets. Oil soaked papers and kindling wood, with candles burning on top of them, were found. Under a bed was a wooden box with a complete "plant" of papers, wood and a candle, the whole being soaked in oil.

The fire had made a good start and would have entirely destroyed the place had it not been for the melting of the water pipes.

Then Assistant Fire Marshal of Brooklyn, Thomas P. Brophy, present incumbent of the office, was assigned to the case, and in the course of investigation came upon a number of circumstances which convinced him that the absent woman had caused the fire. In the first place she had had a previous fire when living in Hoyt Street, and on that occasion had accused a certain man of "burning her out." The man had been arrested, but there was not sufficient evidence to hold him. The Fire Marshal had entertained suspicions any way that the accused man was not the person actually guilty.

SUSPICIOUS ACTIONS PREVIOUS TO FIRE

A few days prior to the last fire the Ackerly woman had turned out of her apartments, without any apparent reason, an old soldier, telling him she could no longer permit him to stay with her. He was a man with a wooden leg. In Mrs. Ackerly's previous fire she had put in a claim against the insurance company for "one wooden leg—value $60," the property of the old veteran, but, curiously enough, he had never been deprived of his artificial limb.

She had removed from her apartments a few days before the fire a large number of her belongings.

The absence of the woman in Port Jefferson lent certain difficulties to the case. In the first place, being outside the jurisdiction of the Brooklyn courts, proceedings could not be brought against her without overcoming legal technicalities. The Assistant Fire Marshal managed to locate the Ackerly woman at her mother's place in Port Jefferson. By intimating to her that her old enemy had again burned her out, and telling her the place was completely gutted, he induced her to return with him to Brooklyn.

Once within the jurisdiction of the courts she was immediately arrested and accused of the crime of setting fire to her place in the night time, when other persons were asleep on the premises—"arson in the first degree."

After a lengthy trial before Judge Norman J. Dike, Annie Ackerly was convicted of arson in the second degree, and sentenced to a fourteen-year term in prison, which she is now serving.

She had a policy of $2,000 on her place at the time, and would have collected it had not the dripping water awakened the family living below her.

The fact that she had obtained money from a previous fire had not deterred Insurance Companies from granting her further "protection."

JUDGE DENOUNCES INCENDIARY IN STRONG LANGUAGE

Judge Dike, in pronouncing sentence on this woman, delivered the following scathing comment:

"*There are certain crimes that are so revolting in their disregard of human life that one wonders at the cold-blooded calculation necessary to perpetrate them. Such a crime is arson* in the first degree, for which crime you were indicted, and for which you have been convicted in a lesser degree after a careful trial—the first woman found guilty of this crime here in twenty years.

"I am convinced that you were responsible for the previous fire in your former home, and, when you found you were not suspected of that crime, you planned this affair, and, at the same time, increased the insurance upon your property.

" When the defendant is a woman, a mother, who, *with fiendish indifference for the lives of two families in her house, with four little children in one, and two in the other, such a deed passes human understanding upon any other hypothesis save that you were capable of becoming a murderess by that midnight fire,* arranged in your rooms with the candles set in the oil-soaked combustibles. You, absent to avoid suspicion, and all for the paltry INSURANCE MONEY you hoped to get.

" I have never seen a cooler, a more calculating prisoner; no womanly sympathy here, simply a fire-fiend trying to secure money at any cost. Any feeling of pity or sympathy for you at this hour I must suspend before my stronger feeling of duty towards the people of this community whose lives and property have twice been in jeopardy through your act.

" You are a menace to this city of homes, and I send you to Auburn prison for a term of not less than fourteen years, and not more than fourteen years and six months."

WOMAN'S CLEVER RUSE

An extremely interesting case in which a woman was concerned—but whose name cannot be mentioned here for certain reasons—occurred in the " Fire Bug Zone " on November 23, 1911. Chief William Guerin, head of the Bureau of Fire Prevention, received information that a certain person would " make a fire " on the date mentioned, at 235 East 105th Street.

" He will not make the fire himself," said the informant, " but his mother-in-law will do it for him. She made the last fire he had. He will make all the arrangements."

Naturally a close watch was kept upon the premises, and a few days prior to the looked-for event, Battalion Chief Howe saw the fire bug bring into the building a load of old furniture on a push-cart. He had an opportunity to inspect closely the furniture, and it showed ample evidence of having been previously burned. It was taken into the building and, of course, was intended to form part of the " exhibits " of damaged stuff which would constitute a claim against the insurance company after the fire, in case the fire did not totally destroy the premises and their contents.

A few minutes before the time set for the fire, Chief Howe saw the wife and children of the fire bug—who had himself gone away—leave the building and go to a moving picture show. Twenty minutes afterwards a boy came running out of the building crying " Fire."

Chief Howe rushed into the building and found the mother-in-law standing in the hall outside the flat (she had been duly announced several days previously as the incendiary) beating on the door and crying " Fire." She stated, on examination afterwards, under oath, that while engaged in the rear of the premises washing she " heard a smell " and went outside into the hall to investigate. While out there the door shut-to, and locked her out.

EVIDENCE OF A " FLASH FIRE "

Firemen entering the room found the heat to be intense—far greater than that which would attend the ordinary burning of household effects. The fire was blazing in a bedroom. It bore all the marks of incendiary origin, and was what might be called technically of the " quick flash " order, having travelled with remarkable swiftness and developed great local intensity; a well recognized feature of incendiary fires where highly inflammable substances are used for the purpose of starting the fire. Though much local destruction occurred immediately at the seat of the origin of the fire, the rest of the furniture was little more than " smoke damaged."

Owing to the suspicious character of this fire, the insurance companies, at the instigation of Fire Marshal John P. Prial, fought the claim put in by these people; and won a suit brought against them for non-payment under the policies. The fire in question had been so carefully planned and carried out that it was not possible at that time to obtain a conviction for arson, though there was not the slightest doubt of the incendiary nature of the blaze.

The claims made against the insurance companies were preposterous on their face, and when the case came up for trial, the jury soon disposed of it, reaching a decision in favor of the companies.

Action should have been brought against these persons both for filing false proofs of loss; and for perjury. The penalty for filing a false proof of loss against an insurance company is imprisonment for 5 years, or a fine of $500, or both. Penalty in perjury cases ranges from 10 to 20 years, according to the nature of the offense.

It might be mentioned that it was the above case which first brought officials of the Fire Department in close contact with the Steinkreutzer affair; as the Harlem fire bug and the "mother-in-law" in this case and her family were closely connected, by ties of what might be called "fire-affinities," if not of blood.

THE MATTIE MICHAELS CASE

Another woman fire bug to receive judicial deserts was Mattie Michaels, a negress, aged 33, who set fire to her place, 207 West 33d Street, Manhattan, at 3.55 A. M., on July 10, 1911. When the firemen reached the scene, they discovered five separate and distinct fires in the building; the place being literally saturated with kerosene oil.

The Michaels woman was seen leaving her place about five minutes prior to the time at which the fire was discovered by a policeman. No one was on the premises, when the fire apparatus arrived.

Though the contents of the premises were valued at about $100, *she had obtained* $3,000 *worth of insurance* a short time before the fire. A few days before the fire, she had removed all of her valuables to a flat in West 59th Street. A month before the fire, she had paid $100 on her furniture, putting up her insurance policy as collateral.

Mattie Michaels was tried twice; the first jury disagreeing. On the second occasion, however, she was sentenced to a prison term of not less than 7 years or more than 15; and is now working out that sentence.

WOMAN INCENDIARY MAKES CONFESSION

Women who undertake the role of fire bugs usually play their parts in such a way as to avoid detection; and doubtless many women in Greater New York have succeeded in having numerous "curtain-and-gas-jet," closet, and kitchen fires, and have frequently collected money from insurance companies.

Sometimes, however, "the best laid plains" miscarry; as was the case in which Mrs. Annie Singer, of 6021 Third Avenue, Brooklyn, figured on the night of August 5, 1910. Here a most elaborate and cleverly planned "plant" not only failed to work but resulted in conviction both of the woman and her co-conspirator, Jacob Ostrinsky.

The discovery of the fire came about in a peculiar way: At 1.04 o'clock on the morning in question, James Wilkie, a motorman on a trolley car, noticed the red glare of a fire from the premises mentioned above, as he was passing by in his car. With commendable curiosity, he stopped and investigated. He saw Mrs. Singer apparently sleeping near the doorway of her shop, with her two children beside her—one an infant in a cradle. It was a hot August night; and the woman had taken up her position near the doorway. The door was about four inches open, so that Wilkie could see through it.

Wilkie saw that two separate fires had started on the woman's left hand side; and he noticed the odor of benzine. Promptly arousing the supposedly sleeping woman, he turned in an alarm. Other tenants in the premises—there were several families with children sleeping above—rushed out; and two of them attempted to put out the fire.

"Don't do that," exclaimed Mrs. Singer, when she saw the efforts of the tenants to put out the flames; "you will only spread the fire. Wait till the firemen come. They can put it out."

DIDN'T WISH FIRE EXTINGUISHED

Mrs. Singer's anxiety not to have the fire extinguished was one of the first facts which directed the suspicions of Fire Marshal Brophy against her.

On arrival of the fire department, the firemen found several wide-mouthed bottles distributed in various parts of the store; and they all contained benzine. A bottle with benzine was also found in one of the rooms in the rear. Around the necks of these bottles, Assistant Fire Marshal Ferris found cords fastened; and these cords led to a main string which passed out to the door where Mrs. Singer pretended to be sleeping.

She claimed not to know anything about the fire; denied any knowledge of the purpose of the bottles or the strings; and suggested that possibly burglars may have entered the place from a rear entrance; as she was accustomed to sleep in the doorway.

A number of suspicious circumstances attracted the attention of the Brooklyn Fire Marshal. In the first place, he ascertained that new shades had recently been purchased and placed in the street windows. He also learned that a strange man had been visiting Mrs. Singer.

Putting all things together, he doubted Mrs. Singer's contentions; and, at Fire Headquarters, after a severe cross-examination, managed to extract a confession from her; declaring that the fire was made by one Jacob Ostrinsky, who lived a short distance away in the immediate neighborhood. She also admitted that she was financially embarrassed, having only 30 cents left. Ostrinsky had advised her to take out an additional fire insurance policy. She also described how they had gone to another locality and rented a store.

CHICAGO INCENDIARY ASSISTS WOMAN

Ostrinsky told Mrs. Singer he had met with great success in Chicago. He had had two fires there; both of which were "profitable." On one occasion, he said the family who gave him the job of making the fire was at the theatre, while, at the other job, he had actually allowed himself to be "rescued" by the Chicago Fire Department. He explained how "easy" it would be to have a fire; and how nobody would ever find it out.

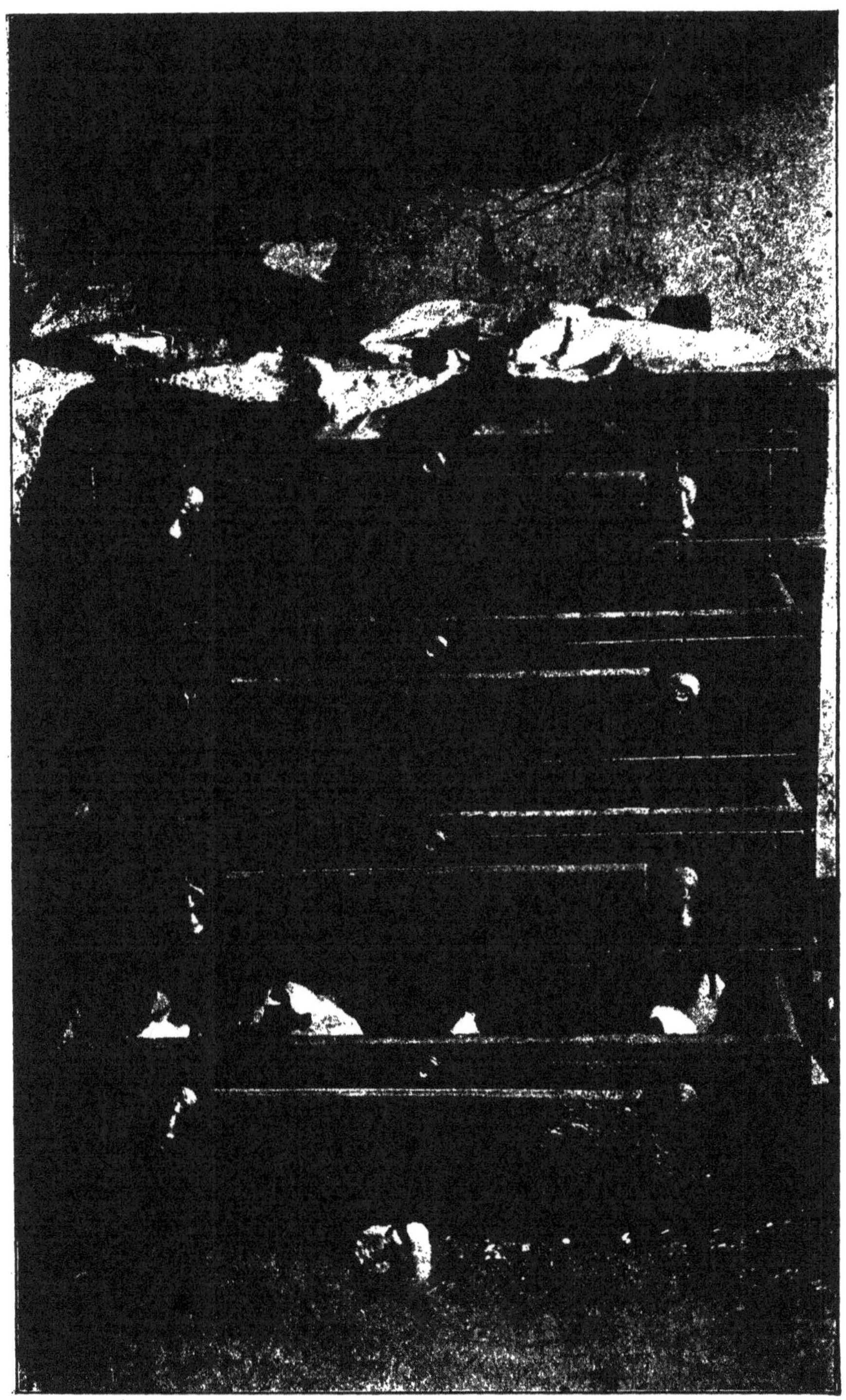

"Plant" in Chiffonier. Note Candle and Drawers Filled with Paper Soaked with Kerosene Oil.

Fire Marshal Brophy finally got in touch with Ostrinsky, who stated that on the day of the fire he had delivered "bread" to the Singer woman. Under cross-examination, he ultimately admitted that the package which he claimed to be a loaf of bread was nothing more or less than a can of benzine. He was found to have delivered this alleged "loaf" a few hours before the fire.

Investigation showed that, less than a month before the fire—on July 13, 1911—Mrs. Singer had taken out an *insurance policy on the store and household effects, in the Commercial Union Assurance Company of London for* $1,300. *This policy was made out to Mrs. Annie Singer, Widow; and was in addition to the policy which her husband—who had died several months previously—had left her in the Fire Association of Philadelphia, for* $1,000.

Owing to the gravity of the crime—several families with little children living in the house over the store, and their lives having been greatly endangered—the fire occurring, as stated, at 1 in the morning—Mrs. Singer was shown—by the Fire Marshal—the inhuman character of her act. She then broke down, and exclaimed:

"I didn't want the fire—I didn't do it. I will tell the truth to show that I made a mistake in being influenced by a bad man. He is a fire bug, and he made fires in Chicago."

Ostrinsky and Mrs. Singer were confronted with each other, and a dramatic scene ensued.

When arraigned in court, each one blamed the other; but finally each pleaded guilty. County Judge Lewis L. Fawcett censured them both in the strongest terms, sentencing Mrs. Singer to two-and-one-half years and not more than five years in Auburn prison; while Jacob Ostrinsky was sent away to Sing Sing for seven and one-half years and not more than fifteen years.

Ostrinsky had only been in these parts three months prior to his capture by the Brooklyn Fire Marshal.

DIFFICULTIES OF CONVICTION IN ARSON CASES

Space does not permit further recital of details of arson cases. There have been many recent trials of incendiaries in which the persons charged have escaped owing to the peculiar character of evidence required in order to bring about conviction. Numbers of cases of undoubted arson cannot be prosecuted owing to lack of technical evidence; though Fire Marshals may know positively who the guilty parties are.

As stated many times in this report, convictions in arson cases are most difficult of attainment; owing to the destruction of material evidence. Incendiaries are well acquainted with these conditions, and take every advantage of them.

Owing to this state of affairs, there is all the more reason why the stamping out of arson should be approached from another direction than that of catching "fire bugs" in the act. This approach must be made from the side of insurance; for, by so doing, the incendiary will be deprived of the principal motive for his act.

CHAPTER IX.

REMEDIES

Insurance Companies Furnish Arson Motive—Stop Indiscriminate Granting of Policies and Incendiarism would Automatically Cease—Recommendations as to Changes in Insurance Methods. Conclusion.

INDISCRIMINATE granting of policies by insurance companies, without proper previous investigation of character of applicant and nature of risk, is the main cause of the crime of arson. Possession of a policy of insurance by the incendiary forms the motive for every such act.

The present system of conducting fire insurance business in this country is responsible for not less than one-fourth—some authorities say more than one-third—of our annual fire-loss.

It also helps to account for the remarkable discrepancies between fire-losses in American cities and those in European communities. London, Paris, Berlin and other foreign cities have but a fraction of the number of fires which afflict American cities.

In London, during 1910, there were 3,941 fires, while New York had 14,405. Paris had but 2,030 fires; Berlin 2,068. Greater New York has 300 fires per 100,000 inhabitants, while London, for the same population, has but 81; Paris, 74; Berlin, 97; Vienna, 59; St. Petersburg, 75.

Our fire-loss per head of population is nearly five times greater than that of any foreign city. In this city, during 1911, our per capita loss was $2.45, while the average for European cities was less than 50 cents. The fire-loss per capita for both Southampton and Dresden was as low as 12 cents.

Incendiarism is largely responsible for these conditions, after making every allowance for the more extensive use of inflammable building materials in this country, and for climatic differences.

We have estimated the percentage of fires due to incendiarism as one-fourth; but experts claim it to be far higher. Mr. F. H. Ross, already referred to as Metropolitan Manager of three large insurance companies, recently wrote a letter to the Fire Commissioner, in which he stated:

> "*After an underwriting experience of 29 years in this city, during all that time having represented companies and adjusted losses, I think 40 per cent., or even higher, would be more correct*" (*for incendiary fires*).
>
> "And then you could add 30 per cent. more of this character: 'accidental' fires, where the assured, after the loss, try to collect from 100 per cent. to 500 per cent. more than the actual loss."

Fire Marshal Thomas P. Brophy, of Brooklyn, as stated, also estimates incendiary fires at about 30 per cent. of the total.

FORTY BILLION DOLLARS AT RISK

In this city, there are about 175 Fire Insurance Companies, with an amount at risk throughout the country of approximately forty billion dollars ($40,000,000,000). The total insurance on actual fire-losses in Greater New York for the year 1911, on the 14,574 fires which occurred, amounted to $331,245,510, while the insurance in force in this city at the present time is estimated at between three and four billion dollars.

Owing to their accumulations of capital, and their great amount at risk, fire insurance companies exert enormous influence—financial and otherwise. As fire insurance closely affects credit, the operations of these companies become a matter of important public interest.

With the fire insurance companies rests the means of removing incendiarism, so far as this evil may be traced to present methods of conducting fire insurance business. These companies have the power to issue or withhold policies; and it devolves upon them to exercise all due diligence in wielding their important responsibility.

It is essential that, in the conduct of fire insurance business, policies shall be issued only to applicants—whether firms or individuals—whose character can bear the fullest scrutiny.

Certain questions are here pertinent:

What steps, if any, do fire insurance companies in this city take to ascertain the exact nature of risks on which they issue policies, or the character and financial standing of persons to whom such policies are granted?

Also: What steps, if any, do these companies take to ascertain the standing and integrity of brokers, agents, and adjusters through whom they conduct a large portion of their business? As the Fire Insurance Exchange issues to brokers annually upwards of 7,500 licenses at $10 each, they have it in their power to see to it that such permits to do business only reach the trustworthy.

Another question:

Are fire insurance companies in America conducting their business in accordance with the best precedents and practices—as exemplified, for instance, by foreign fire insurance companies operating abroad?

COMPANIES STRICT ABROAD—CARELESS HERE

All foreign fire insurance companies doing business in this country—and there are many large concerns—conduct their American affairs on lines wholly different from those pursued by the same companies abroad.

In no European city would insurance be granted on the same conditions upon which it is freely given in Greater New York.

European fire insurance companies do business here on principles contrary to those pursued by the same companies in their own land. Together with American companies, they take every advantage of all the latitude allowed by law.

In the absence of legal restraints, the obligation of the companies is at present wholly moral. But this fact enhances, rather than minimizes, the responsibility which rests upon them.

During the course of this investigation, an opportunity of obtaining an insight into foreign insurance methods was afforded by the visit of Mr. Robert H. Mainzer to Germany. Mr. Mainzer obtained, for the New York Fire Department, valuable data concerning the system employed by German Fire Insurance Companies prior to issuing policies. His report is as follows:

REPORT OF MR. ROBERT H. MAINZER ON METHODS OF GERMAN FIRE INSURANCE COMPANIES

"New York, October 5, 1912.

"Hon. JOSEPH JOHNSON,
"Fire Commissioner,
"New York City.

"My dear Commissioner:

"In accordance with the request expressed by you before my departure for Europe, I have the honor and pleasure to report to you that I have made as thorough an investigation and study into German Fire Insurance Companies as can be made in the short space of about four weeks. I chose the German Fire Insurance Companies as models, as I found that their restrictions were the most severe, and the German law on the subject the most stringent and carefully worded. In this connection, I am sending you herewith two volumes giving you: (1), the laws for private insurance companies, and (2), the imperial laws on insurance contracts.

"In the course of conversation both with the directors of leading insurance companies and with parties who have occasion to require a great deal of insurance, I learned that the latter class is usually rather at the mercy of the former. A gentleman who recently had to insure various industrial plants tells me that the German Insurance Companies always stipulate that, no matter what amount of insurance is taken out, the damage is appraised in their own certain way by the *company,* and not more than the actual damage is reimbursed. It is further stipulated that the damages paid by the company have to be used to replace the damaged plant or machinery, etc. According to his experience, the methods pursued by fire insurance companies in Germany are not at all encouraging to people who lack 'moral responsibility,' as we call it. In fact, he informed me that the laws are not very encouraging even to legitimate insurers, owing to the severe clauses of the contracts and the many difficulties encountered in recovering on properly incurred fire-damage. Various informants seemed to agree that in negotiating for fire insurance they were absolutely in the hands of the insurance companies.

"I am sending you herewith a large number of pamphlets, containing not only the great number of questions, which the party has to answer when he applies for insurance, but also the confidential communications made by the agent or insurance broker to the company, regarding the party wanting insurance. All these answers are scrupulously examined before any policy is issued. I have endeavored to translate these many questions, which run into the greatest detail on every conceivable subject, with a strict adherence to the German text, and you will at once note the most exacting search into your past, present, and even future, which you must submit to before the insurance company will write any policy.

"In addition, I learned that in most German cities a system of Industrial Police (Gewerbepolizei) is maintained, which sees to it that the insured party strictly adheres to every detail of the factory laws. This is an additional safeguard for the insurance companies after the policy is written.

"My conclusion is that in Germany the law, as written, is universally obeyed, and is not written to be broken as often as possible.

The Germans adhere to the spirit as well as to the letter of the law. Very few men in Germany will take the chance of having the government shut down their factory for an indeterminate period for violating the stringent factory laws.

"I found that there was no maximum amount fixed on any one square block in any of the larger cities, but each insurance company knows exactly how much insurance it will carry on a certain block; and, as the companies work hand in hand in a kind of pool, they need never fear any over-insurance on any block. In fact, their *rigid system of inspection before writing a policy,* an inspection made by men who are experts on every line of goods that they inspect, precludes the idea of over-insurance. This *thorough system of inspection* makes it quite clear that it rarely pays to set fire to your premises or your factory. I understand that such cases are of rarest occurrence.

"There is no doubt in my mind that the thorough inspection coupled with the most stringent laws on every conceivable kind of motive power, electric and gas lighting, etc., together with the drastic building laws, are the reasons for the comparatively few fires that occur in German cities.

"I am enclosing the laws laid down for various motors and lighting systems, which will show you the force of my argument. This data may be useful for the Bureau of Fire Prevention. From personal observation and talks with men engaged in this system of inspection, I find that the quality of men employed counts far more than the quantity.

"Much more could be written on this subject, but I have tried to touch upon the most salient points only, and in mere outline at that.

"In summing up, I would say that if you want to see a reduction in the number of fires in New York, you would have to put through:

"1. Legislation compelling the American Fire Insurance Companies to write their policies on the lines laid down by the German companies, demanding exact answers to the questions, as per enclosures, and *discriminating carefully in accepting risks.*

"2. *More rigid inspection than in vogue now* of all buildings by thorough men trained by years of experience in this line of business.

"3. Much more rigid building, especially factory laws, which must be obeyed to the letter, or the premises shut down.

"I also wish to state that I have carefully inspected the Motor Fire apparatus of all the larger cities in Germany, Holland, Belgium and France, and will make a verbal report on this inspection whenever you wish me to do so. Inasmuch as many of the European departments used motors long before we did, their experience should be of value to us.

"With the sincere hope that I have been of some service to you in this matter, and that you will also transmit these lines with the enclosures to Chief John Kenlon, I beg to remain,

"Yours respectfully,

"(Signed) ROBERT H. MAINZER."

QUESTIONS ASKED BY GERMAN COMPANIES

The first sentence in the German Fire Insurance Laws reads: *"Insurance should not lead to the enrichment of the assured,"* and it is on these lines that policies are issued throughout the German Empire. The number and intimacy of the questions asked leave no loophole for fraud or deception.

When an applicant has passed the fire insurance inquisition in Germany, it is safe to say that he is fully entitled to his policy.

To cite a few questions asked the assured by *The Providentia,* one of the largest German companies:

> Question. To whom do the articles to be insured belong?
>
> Q. *Has the applicant ever had a fire before? If so, state when, where, giving full particulars.*
>
> Q. Have the articles for which insurance is desired ever been insured before; if so, state in what companies.
>
> Q. If the party has had a former fire, *what insurance was collected;* state full particulars as to fire, its nature, origin, and what damages were collected.
>
> Q. *Give full particulars as to financial standing.*

In addition to many other questions of the most searching kind, the *agent who obtains the application must give a personal warranty* to the company that the business is desirable. He must also sign a Report of Inspection which leaves nothing hidden. Among other things, such questions as the following must be answered by the agent, who is also a skilled inspector:

> Q. What could you ascertain about the moral character and financial condition of the applicant?
>
> Q. *Is the applicant known to you personally* as a decent individual and does he enjoy a good reputation?
>
> Q. *Can you recommend our granting this insurance* with the absolute conviction that we are acting for our best interests, after you have conscientiously examined the request, and after going into all conditions most carefully?
>
> Q. Do you believe, leaving out all considerations of friendship and personal interest, that the company would do a desirable business by accepting this insurance?

In answer to a number of questions as to their manner of conducting fire insurance, the Prussian National Insurance Company of Stettin, stated, among other things:

> "Applications for insurance on furniture and household effects are usually made up by the agents or other employees of the company, *when visiting the risk offered.*"

It will thus be seen that previous personal inspection of risks is one of the ordinary means employed by companies in Germany in placing insurance. These companies, however, issue policies in New York without any such precautions. (See lists, pp. 31, 34, 35, 36, 38, 39, 40, 41, 42.)

To the question: "In paying losses after fires, what steps do you take, if any, to prevent fraud, or the collection of insurance through fraudulent methods?" the following significant answer was given by the Prussian National Insurance Company:

> "Company is not allowed to pay any claim on household furniture before previous advice to the police."

FOREIGN COMPANIES EXPLAIN THEIR METHODS

In addition to the German companies, information was obtained by correspondence from the following other foreign fire insurance companies:

Atlas Assurance Company of London, England;
Alliance Insurance Company, of London;
British American Assurance Company, Toronto, Canada;
Caledonian Insurance Company, Edinburgh, Scotland;
Commercial Union Assurance Company, Liverpool, England;
Century Insurance Company, of Edinburgh, Scotland;
Liverpool and London and Globe Insurance Co., Liverpool;
North British and Mercantile Insurance Co., London;
Northern Assurance Company, London;
Norwich Union Fire Insurance Society, Norwich, England;
Royal Exchange Assurance Company, London;
Scottish Union and National Insurance Company, Edinburgh;
Sun Insurance Company, London;
Svea Fire and Life Insurance Company, Gothenburg, Sweden;
Yorkshire Insurance Company, York, England;
Phoenix Assurance Company, London, England.

Though all of above companies, in their replies, showed that their methods of inquiry and inspection before issuing policies are very strict and thorough in their own country, yet, with few exceptions, none follows the same precautions in this city. All but three of above companies granted policies without previous investigation to members of the Fire Department on valueless household effects at various places in this city.

Here are a few answers to questions put to some of the companies named above:

THE BRITISH AMERICAN ASSURANCE COMPANY, OF TORONTO, when asked what steps are taken on receipt of an application for insurance, replied:

> " Nearly all such applications come through agents and it is their duty *to inspect, and learn the exact nature of every risk they send in, including the character and standing of the applicant. The agent is expected to make personal inspection whether amounts involved are large or small."*

In reply to the question: " What steps, if any, are taken by your company, to prevent, or forestall, the commission of arson with a view to the collection of insurance money?" the following answer was given by the company above mentioned:

> " The greatest protection is *to see that the amount of insurance is kept within the actual value of the property so that a margin of the value may be left as a responsibility upon the assured. This has the effect of encouraging the care, rather than the destruction of the property."*

Replying to the query: " What specific steps does your company take, if any, to prevent applicants from over-insuring," the following answer was made:

> " *The character of applicant and the value of property seeking insurance are the first things to be considered,* and the company in one way or another gets what it considers satisfactory evidence on

those points before accepting the risk. *Inspection by agents and company's officials are the chief means of protection against over-insurance."*

The LIVERPOOL AND LONDON AND GLOBE INSURANCE COMPANY OF LIVERPOOL, which does a large fire insurance business in Greater New York, gave, through its New York Manager, Mr. Henry W. Eaton, replies to the following questions, as to its methods of doing business *abroad:*

> Q. "On receipt of an application by the company or its agent for insurance on furniture or household effects, what steps, if any, does your company or agent, take to ascertain the exact nature of the risk; and what inquiry, if any, is made as to the character or standing of the applicant?
>
> A. "Report of agent is required *as to character or standing; and, in other than small insurances a superficial inspection is made."*
>
> Q. "What steps, if any, are taken by your company to prevent or forestall the commission of arson with a view to the collection of insurance money?
>
> A. "None beyond *precaution in acceptance."*

It is somewhat singular that though this company uses care and takes precautions in issuing policies *abroad,* yet it accepts risks in Greater New York, and even in hazardous districts (see pp. 31 and 32 of this report) without question. Inspection of the lists on the pages mentioned will show that the Liverpool and London and Globe Fire Insurance Company, through agents in this city, issued three separate policies, amounting to $2,000 on less than $4 worth of property at 239 East 101st Street, Borough of Manhattan, and without any inspection whatever; or inquiry as to character or standing of applicant; and even without filling a proposal form, such as is universally required by all foreign companies abroad.

REQUIREMENTS OF FOREIGN FIRE INSURANCE

"Proposal forms" are invariably required in all cases of persons applying for insurance in British and German companies; furthermore, all companies require that their agents, in taking the insurance, shall give in writing a personal recommendation of the business.

If agents abroad recommend business of a risky character they are effectively "blacklisted" among all companies. In this country, as has been shown, if an agent or broker succeeds in doing a certain amount of business, he is permitted to accept risks known to be dubious. (See this Report, p. 38.)

In this connection, the answer of the NORWICH UNION FIRE INSURANCE COMPANY—one of the largest foreign companies, is interesting:

The question was put: "What steps, if any, are taken by your company to prevent, or forestall, the commission of arson, with a view to the collection of insurance money?"

> "Answer: *Cases of arson* are in our experience *of very rare occurrence, which fact we believe to be due to the care exercised in the selection of business by our Branch Managers and agents who have in most instances a personal knowledge of the proposer."*

As will be seen by inspection of list on page 31 of this Report, the Norwich Union Fire Insurance Company also issued insurance without inspection in the "Fire Bug Zone"—on property at 239 East 101st Street, Borough of Manhattan, giving $500 on less than $4 worth of property.

Space does not permit citation of all questions asked both would-be assurers and agents by all foreign companies, but a few selections from some of the various proposal forms might be here introduced:

FURTHER QUESTIONS ASKED APPLICANTS

Questions put to the proposer by the Northern Assurance Company of London, are: "How long have you resided in the premises referred to?" "On whose recommendation have you applied to the 'Northern?' If not that of an agent or client of the company, please give name and address of a reference?"

THE ALLIANCE ASSURANCE COMPANY, OF LONDON, says, to its agents: "The Directors trust that the Company's *agents will systematically reject all proposals from parties whose character is in the slightest degree questionable.*" They also ask the agents: "How long have you known the proposer?" "Has a fire occurred in any premises occupied by the owner or occupier or either of them; and if so, when, where, and in what office assured?"

THE CENTURY INSURANCE COMPANY OF EDINBURGH, asks:

"Are you at present insured in this or any other office? If so, please state particulars?" Also, "Have you ever had a fire, either in these premises or elsewhere? If so, state particulars?"

THE ROYAL EXCHANGE ASSURANCE COMPANY OF LONDON, besides asking questions as outlined above, demand of its agents:

> "*Are you personally acquainted with the Proposer?*
>
> "Is the proposal one that you feel fully justified in recommending the Corporation to accept?"
>
> "Do you consider the *amounts proposed a fair insurable* value for the property?"

THE SCOTTISH UNION AND NATIONAL COMPANY OF EDINBURGH, asks its agents: "Are the proposer and the occupants of the premises *thoroughly respectable?*" "Has the insurance been declined by any insurance company?" "Does the value of the property, in your opinion, warrant the amount of insurance?" "Have you inspected the property?" "What is the distance to the nearest fire-engine station?" "*Do you recommend the Directors to undertake the Insurance?*" "Has the proposer ever had a fire on these or other premises?"

Besides asking the questions required on the usual "proposal form," and laying particular emphasis on the matter of "previous fires," the PHOENIX ASSURANCE COMPANY OF LONDON inserts this clause as the first condition of its policy:

"*If there shall have been any material misdescription of any of the property hereby insured or of any building or place in which any such property is contained, or any misrepresentation as to or omission to state any fact material to be known for estimating the risk,* the Company shall not be liable upon this policy so far as it relates to the property affected by such misdescription, misrepresentation or omission, and if there has been *any misstatement in answer to questions put by or on behalf of the Company on the proposal for the insurance the Company shall not be liable upon this policy."*

THE ATLAS ASSURANCE COMPANY OF LONDON, puts this question to its agents: "Is the proposer known to you of *good character and in satisfactory circumstances?"* It also asks many questions both of agent and proposer, one being: "Have you ever made a claim against an insurance company? If so, please give particulars?" The agent is also required to sign a statement saying: "I recommend acceptance of the proposal."

THE SUN FIRE OFFICE OF LONDON, requires to know, among many other things: "Has a fire occurred in any building whilst wholly or partially occupied by you?"

FOREIGN COMPANIES "BLACKLIST" APPLICANTS

A question asked the ATLAS ASSURANCE COMPANY OF LONDON—one of the largest companies—was as follows:

> "Have you any central bureau utilized by all companies, where suspicious fires are reported; and where records are kept of persons who have had previous fires?"

To which they replied:

> "No—except to a limited extent. But *companies freely exchange information which is often the means of learning who are undersirable applicants."*

This company insists in all cases upon the character and standing of the applicant being fully disclosed and known to be good. The applicant must give a reference, and the agent must recommend the risk.

Though certain variations exist among the different proposal forms used by foreign fire insurance companies, all of them insist upon two essential points: Responsibility of the agent guaranteeing the character of assured; and specific answer to the question as to previous fires.

In this country, none of the companies inquires into the *character of applicants*; nor do the occurrence of previous fires deter companies from granting policies. In fact, the report of the New York Board of Fire Underwriters for 1911, already cited, distinctly states that 37.6 per cent. in number of incurred losses during the year were from "*assured who have had previous losses adjusted by this Committee."*

This report further states: "Our past year's work shows a very large increase in number and amount of losses incurred, with *a large number of suspicious fires*, in many cases *involving more or less evident moral hazard."* And further, the same report says: "We have in hand under investigation or adjustment many more claims of this character than have ever been in our hands at one time before."

DO COMPANIES WISH TO PREVENT ARSON?

Despite the situation which confronts the insurance people in the matter of increased incendiary fires, it never seems to occur to them that there might be something radically wrong with methods of doing insurance business in this country.

There are about forty-five (45) large foreign companies with branch agencies in Greater New York, who seek business without adopting any of the safeguards which their home offices follow abroad. Insurance is accepted by most of these companies without any inspection whatever nor are agents required to supply any "certificate of character," as to applicants.

From time to time, among insurance authorities, discussions are held as to the best methods of suppressing the crime of arson, and rewards are even offered for the apprehension of criminals. In fact, since 1873, the National Board of Fire Underwriters has offered rewards for convictions in arson and incendiary cases, amounting to the considerable sum of $2,004,075. Though such a large sum has been *offered* throughout this thirty-nine-year period, it is somewhat significant that only $84,619 has *actually been paid.*

The easiest way to stop arson is to make it unprofitable.

Insurance companies in this country can do this by following the same methods as those pursued by foreign companies. Shutting down on the wholesale granting of policies will make it unnecessary for Insurance Boards of Underwriters to offer rewards.

As with most remedies, the onlv one which suits such crying evils is to lay the axe to the root of the tree. Palliative measures will, as always, prove fruitless.

ARSON FOR INSURANCE MONEY CAN BE STOPPED TOMORROW BY CUTTING OFF THE SOURCE WHENCE INSURANCE MONEY COMES—NAMELY, INSURANCE POLICIES.

The catching of fire bugs—even "in the act"—only deals with individuals, after all. What is needed is a removal of the cause, or inducement, which actuates the incendiary. The motive for arson, as stated so often throughout this Report, is insurance. Stop insurance of this kind and arson automatically ceases.

REMEDY KNOWN TO ALL

The remedy here suggested is universally known by all insurance companies doing business in this country. Doubtless, the adoption of foreign methods prior to the granting of insurance would make inroads into profits; but, where one class of business would and *should* be lost, better risks would equalize this loss, for it is an axiom of insurance that the better the class of risk, the higher the insurance profit.

In fact, if arson for insurance money were done away with, greater security for all risks would naturally result.

The companies need not necessarily lose business. It might be contended that it would be impossible to do business at the same low rates as now exist. The answer is: Foreign companies do the same class of business at very low rates and manage to pay very substantial dividends.

In this connection, the words of the Manager of the Sun Insurance Office, London—one of the largest English companies—might be quoted. In a letter to Acting Chief William Guerin, head of the BUREAU OF FIRE PREVENTION, he wrote, when answering certain questions.

"You may perhaps think that business on this side is conducted in somewhat easy-going fashion, but the results justify our methods as shown *by the low rates chargeable* and the satisfactory results of the business." The Sun Office has been in business since 1710.

If this and other companies can do business, and be free from incendiarism, no reason whatever exists why companies, operating in this country, should not follow foreign precedents.

Until some such changes in the methods of granting insurance are made, naturally our fire bugs will take advantage of the temptation held out to them.

It might be contended that this argument does not apply to the merchant insuring a stock of goods, with the intention of taking advantage of a fire. Were our insurance companies here to follow the minute inspection and character tests pursued by the German companies, it is safe to say that ninety per cent. (90%) of this type of " business " fires would be prevented.

It will be necessary before bringing about the reforms advocated in this Report, to obtain the enactment of certain legislative measures restricting and regulating insurance companies in this country.

RECOMMENDATIONS

The following proposals, as to changes in Fire Insurance methods are recommended:

I. Amendment of present Standard Fire Insurance Policy, so as to conform, in all respects, to the most stringent regulations of Foreign Policies.

II. Limitation of insurance where applicants have had previous suspicious fires.

III. Cancellation of policies, in suspicious cases, at instance of Fire Commissioner. Powers given to Fire Commissioner to veto licenses of dishonest brokers, agents and adjusters.

IV. Rigid inventory of stock in all cases and notice of substantial decrease served on companies by applicant under penalty of Policy becoming void. Prohibition of reduction of stock below certain percentage (say, 25%) without notification to Companies.

V. Assured having more than three fires, after which insurance was collected, to be compelled to obtain certificate of character from Fire Marshal showing assured to be without suspicion.

VI. Rigid prior inspection of all property in accordance with Foreign system of Proposal Forms (This is included in Clause 1, but needs specific emphasis).

VII. All answers by assured on Proposal Forms to become warranties in Policy; any false or misleading statements thereupon to vitiate contract.

VIII. Insurance to be limited to actual value.

IX. Central Bureau of Information for use of Fire Insurance Companies to be established at Fire Headquarters in which will be kept on file, for immediate reference by Companies, names of all parties having suspicious fires. This Bureau to be used by all Insurance Companies before granting policies.

X. Inspection of Books of suspected firms and individuals by Fire Department to ascertain Financial Conditions of all such suspected persons applying for Fire Insurance.

XI. Publicity of all Cases of Fires where Cause of same is "Not Ascertained," and where fires are suspicious in origin.

XII. Active co-operation among Fire Department, Police Department, State Banking Department, and State Insurance Department as to the granting of insurance; the licensing of brokers, and adjusters; and in the investigation of character of suspected persons applying for Fire Insurance.

APPENDIX "A"

SHOWING GERMAN METHOD OF INQUIRY INTO APPLICATIONS FOR INSURANCE

TRANSLATED FOR THE

NEW YORK FIRE DEPARTMENT

BY

MR. ROBERT H. MAINZER

QUESTIONS ASKED BY GERMAN INSURANCE COMPANIES AND WHICH MUST BE ANSWERED BY ALL APPLICANTS BEFORE POLICIES ARE ISSUED

Request for Insurance for Factories

I

We the undersigned..
living in..................................request from the Providentia, Frankfurt Insurance Co. in Frankfurt, under the known usual conditions and under the specially mentioned conditions in connection with the policy requested, promising to answer exactly the following questions and any others which might be demanded—fire insurance on the following objects:

QUESTIONS, WHICH THE APPLICANT MUST ANSWER

Property and Ownership Conditions

Who is the owner of the factory for which insurance is wanted?
Who is at the head of the business (owner, leased or director)?
Who is the owner of the objects to be insured?

You must mention here whether work is done entirely or partly for other people or for wages.

All objects which belong to others must be mentioned as such.

Besides the party asking for insurance, have other parties any use of any of the shops or machines by lease or otherwise? If so, state all particulars.

Location

Where is the factory? Place....................District...................
Street..................No.......................

Structural Conditions

How old are the buildings?

Were the buildings erected for the present purpose or for what were they used formerly?

Do the separate buildings consist oi basement without cellar and without attic?

What buildings or parts of buildings are separated from each other by fire walls? (You may only consider as fire walls absolutely massive partition walls which are at least 30 cm. strong at the peak of the roof, which cut through the wooden construction of the roof attic and which protrude at least 30 cm. over the roof.)

Are there openings in these fire walls? Where? Can they be closed by iron doors or shutters—safe against fire?

What rooms are arched? Are the arches made of stone or of stone and iron? Of what material are the supports of the arches?

What rooms have other fireproof ceilings and of what kind are the latter?

Which have wooden ceilings?

What rooms have floors of fireproof material and what kind of material?

Are rooms lying above one another connected by openings or shafts or elevators, and state the buildings in which this is the case?

Of what material are the stairs and how wide are they? Are the stairs in a separate stair-house and how is it built?

Are there any connecting passageways or bridges or galleries? Of what material? Are the doors which lead to these bridges or galleries of iron?

Motive Power

Is there hand or machine power? What is the motive power of the machines (steam, electricity, gas, hot air, animal, wind, water, etc.)?

How many workmen are employed?

What motors (steam, gas) are there and how many?

How many boilers and what system are they?

Are the boilers and motors in special buildings or are they in the factory buildings and in which?

Is the cover of the steam pipes of fireproof material? Name the material.

Are all the steam pipes (even those for heating the rooms) which are not covered by fireproof material distant at least 5 cm. from all objects which can be ignited?

Heating

Which rooms are heated by steam or hot water and where is the boiler room?

Which rooms are heated by hot air?

Where is the apparatus that generates the hot air? Are these places protected by fireproof floors and walls? Are they arched?

Is the heated air led through canals or pipes into the rooms?

Are the hot-air pipes used entirely or partly to carry off smoke?

Are the hot-air flues or pipes or any accumulators for hot air made of fireproof material? Name it.

Are the hot-air flues and pipes, including the smoke flues, all over—that is, where they go through walls and ceilings too—at least 30 cm. distant from all woodwork and other objects that can catch fire?

Are the hot-air openings covered by fine mesh wire screens?

What rooms are heated by stoves?

Of what material are the stoves?

Do the stoves stand on fireproof supports? What kind of supports?

Are the stoves heated from interior or exterior?

Are the stoves and the flues—also where they go through walls and ceilings—at least 30 cm. away from all woodwork?

What is the length of the chimney flues and do they end in massive chimneys or where do they go?

What precautions are there to prevent ignition of easily inflammable materials at the stoves or by coals which drop out?

Illumination

electric

What rooms are lighted by electricity and state kind of light—arc, etc.?

Who made the lighting apparatus—what system?

Are the dynamos on entirely fireproof material?

Are the switches made of fireproof material? If not, are the various switches mounted on fire proof material (slate, marble, porcelain, asbestos)?

Are the arclights entirely closed below?

Is there a regular inspection of the electric installation made by a person thoroughly conversant with all details and if so, how often?

What kind of emergency or reserve illumination is there?

in the latter case

What rooms are lighted by gas?

If the Gas Is Generated in the Factory

What kind are the gas generators?

Where is the apparatus situated and where is the gas tank?

Of what material is the gas made?

What rooms are lighted by fat-oil?

What rooms are lighted by mineral oil and what kind?

What is the maximum amount of mineral oil which is kept on hand?

Where is it stored and how is the storeroom constructed? How is the storeroom separated from other rooms in the factory? How far away is it?

Where are the lamps polished and filled?

Are the lamps lit on the places where they are fastened? Are they always fastened while they are burning or are they used to light up or around the rooms?

Are the flames open or enclosed in cylinders or lamps?

Are the flames at least 1 meter above and 30 cm. at the sides distant from all woodwork, especially wooden ceilings and all other inflammable material?

If this is not the case, how far away are they and what precautionary measures are taken?

What kind of lighting is there in those rooms in which inflammable gases (vapors) or dustlike particles can mix with the air in such a way that an explosion may occur? Is the illumination from without or how?

Are there set rules for looking after the lighting? Is it left to a responsible party (make sure of this)?

Incendiary Fire in Moving Picture Theatre, 408-410 East 116th Street, Manhattan, August 24, 1911. Oil-Filled Bladders Found in Many Places.

Occupation

What is made in the factory?

For what is each building used? (This need not be answered if the answer can be seen from the description above.)

What materials are used to work with?

Is there sorting, cleaning, cutting and mixing of materials and in what buildings?

What products are made?

Are the workshops and packing rooms cleaned daily? Especially is inflammable material, like sawdust, paper clippings, etc., taken away at least once daily from the workshops and where is all refuse carried to?

Are all rags used to clean the machines always kept in fireproof boxes and burned after use or put aside where they will cause no danger?

Is there work at night?

In addition to above heating is there any other method of heating for factory purposes?

What objects are burned, cooked or heated?

In what way?

In what rooms?

How are the heating plants constructed?

Installation for Drying

Is there any drying? What objects are dried and in what manner?

In what buildings and on what floors are the drying rooms?

Are the drying rooms arched massively and have they iron doors?

How are they separated from other rooms?

What kind of heating and lighting is there in the drying rooms?

Up to what temperature are the drying rooms heated?

What material does the drying apparatus consist of—supports, etc.?

Are all drying installations distant at least 1 meter above and 60 cm. at the sides from all heating apparatus?

What precautions are taken, so that articles to be dried cannot drop off and ignite on the heating apparatus?

Are special drying stoves or other drying apparatus used? What kind are they, in what rooms are they and how are they constructed?

Is there any stacking or drying of inflammable material over or next to the boilers?

Is there any carpentering and what kind (state exactly)?

In what buildings does it take place and how separated from other buildings?

What kind of heating in these shops?

If stove heating, is the stove protected by an iron or stone mantle above the flue?

What woodworking machines and how many are in use—saws, etc.?

Is there wood drying in heated rooms, in what rooms and in what way?

Is there any burning or branding of barrels and in what rooms?

Is there any use made of remnants and in what rooms?

In addition to the prescribed line of business is there any side line in the factory—what is it and in which rooms?

In addition to the articles insured, are any others stored in the buildings, and if so in which buildings?

Does the factory use or store varnish, tar, benzine, petroleum or other mineral oils, alcohol, ether oils or other easily inflammable objects? Are materials used, made or stored which are subject to explosion or spontaneous combustion? If so, what kind of materials, for what purpose, in what way and in what rooms?

How are the latter constructed and how are they separated from the rest of the buildings?

Are mineral, vegetable or mixed oils used to oil the machines or materials? Are fatty materials stored?

Is there any other source which might add to the danger or are there any conditions present which might increase the risk and which have not been covered by our questions? What precautions have been taken to avoid consequences?

Patrol

Is there a watchman at night, on holidays and in the daily hours of recess? Only on the outside or also inside the factory? Are there special watchmen for this patrol?

How are the watchmen controlled?

Is there a special set of rules for the patrol?

Means of Putting Out Fires

Has the factory its own water supply system?

If so, how many hydrants?

Has it its own engines—how many?

Has it fire extinguishers and how many?

What other appliances are there for putting out fires?

What help can be expected from outside sources in case of fire and in what time?

Is there always sufficient water near the factory and how far distant?

How many engines are there in the village within a radius of a half-hour?

Neighborhood

How are the neighboring houses built and roofed?

Are they right next door or how far away?

Are there fire walls without openings?

What is the occupation in the neighboring houses?

Within a radius of 60 metres of the factory are there other factories, mills, theatres, wheat, fodder or straw warehouses, coal or wood pockets or other storehouses for dangerous goods or buildings with bad roofs?

Which of these dangers are present and how far away are they?

Insurance Conditions

Were the goods to be insured already insured? In what companies, in what sums and what premium?

If the insurance was with the Providentia, in what policy?

After the insurance started with the Providentia, was insurance taken out in another company in addition? In what companies? What amounts—what premium? Is there insurance on other objects in the factory? If so, on what objects, what amounts and in what companies?

Explosion Insurance

Is this insurance only asked for or against fire or should explosion of the boilers be included? In the latter case, do they want insurance on all or part of the goods?

Do they want insurance against explosion of other than the boilers and which apparatus?

Are the machines supplied with manometers and safety valves?

Is the party a member of a boiler inspection company; if so, which one?

Former Fires

Has the party ever been hit by a former fire or explosion or attempt at arson—if so, how often and when?

At the time what company carried the insurance? Were damages asked for and paid and how much?

Termination

Does the party wish this contract renewed for the same period as this one without further notice, unless either of the parties gives notice in writing four weeks ahead of the termination of the policy?

(If answered affirmatively the Company will renew the policy in time.)

REPORT OF INSPECTION TO BE MADE OUT BY THE SPECIAL AGENT OF GERMAN INSURANCE COMPANIES AFTER QUESTIONS HAVE BEEN ANSWERED BY APPLICANT AS OUTLINED IN FOREGOING STATEMENT

QUESTIONS

What branches of manufacture are carried on on the premises?

In this connection do actual conditions agree with those mentioned in the request for insurance and those in the policy?

Incendiary Fire in Living-rooms Above Moving Picture Show, 408-410 East 116th Street. Note Oil-Filled Bladder in Doorway, Burst Bladder on Floor, Cotton Trailer from Handle of Door. Thirty Bladders Used, each Containing a Gallon of Kerosene Oil.

What impression does the factory make in regard to interior and exterior construction?

How is it situated in regard to nearness of other buildings or people and what help can be expected in case of fire?

What do you think of the factory as a whole and the way it is fitted up?

Is there lots of room?

Do you find order and cleanliness?

What is the connection between each floor and each workshop?

Is each room easily accessible in case of fire?

Is it to be expected that if a fire starts only a part of the factory would be apt to be destroyed or must we fear a total loss?

What are your reasons for either belief?

Has the factory its own fire apparatus and describe it?

What kind of a heating plant has it?

Describe the heating apparatus.

If they have a furnace, what precautions have been taken at the pipes to prevent a fire starting?

Have they any kind of drying apparatus? How is it constructed?

How is the heating of the drying rooms effected?

How is the factory lighted?

Describe the entire lighting apparatus.

Are the flames enclosed in cylinders or lamps?

Are the gas jets sufficiently separated from the ceilings or wooden partitions and are the latter protected by horizontal pieces of metal or otherwise?

Are the lamps fastened or are portable lamps also in use?

How is the factory watched, not only during working hours, but also during hours of rest and at night?

Is there a laid-down rule for watching the factory?

Is there any side occupation in the factory?

If there is any carpenter work are the prescribed conditions lived up to?

What could you find out about the morality (moral character) and the financial condition of the owner?

What is the relation of the owner or directors to the workmen?

How does the factory pay, anyway what do people think about the way the outfit is run and its financial condition?

Do you consider the insurance we wrote on the factory a good one, or what cause may there be to hesitate about the entire matter?

Accordingly, should the insurance be renewed or shall we let it run out?

In the former case do you think the premium proportionate to the risk or shall we work for a higher premium and up to how much?

Do you consider the precautionary measure required in the policy sufficient or do you think changes should be required—state them?

CONFIDENTIAL COMMUNICATION CONCERNING THE APPLICANT

(To be signed by Agent)

Did the requested insurance exist or does it exist with another company? With which company? At what premium? Did the company mentioned stop the insurance or take it up and for what reason?

Did you see the actual premiums paid on the certificate of insurance or how did you find out about them?

Were there any difficulties in regulating the amount of damages to be paid the insured if he had any previous fire or fires?

Is it known to you whether any other company was asked to take this risk? Which one? What premium was asked? Was the insurance refused by any other company and if so why?

Is the man asking for the insurance known to you personally as a decent individual and does he enjoy a good reputation?

Is the man asking for insurance in good circumstances—do you think that he can live on the business he is now doing?

Are you fully convinced that his requests are absolutely in proportion to actual conditions?

Are the buildings to be insured in good structural condition or would you consider them neglected? About how old are the premises to be insured? Do you know the premises from personal inspection?

How did you happen to get the request for insurance? Did you take up the whole question on the spot in person?

Can you recommend our giving this insurance with the absolute conviction that we are acting for our best interests, after you have conscientiously examined the request and after going into all conditions most carefully?

Can you also obtain the burglary insurance on these premises? What company has given a burglary insurance policy and how long does it run?

FURTHER SPECIAL AND CONFIDENTIAL COMMUNICATIONS IN CONNECTION WITH FACTORY INSURANCE APPLICATION

1.

Where is the establishment?

2.

Since when does it exist?

3.

a) Is it in flourishing condition?
b) How do you come to this conclusion?
(Can you find out where the output goes and what connection it has with other important houses?)

4.

Who owns the establishment?

In Case It Belongs to One Person or Actual Partners

5.

a) What do you know about the circumstances of the partners?
b) Do they positively enjoy universal respect and entire confidence in their character?
c) Are they on good footing with their employees?
d) Do they principally work with their own means and is their money not tied up in any way?
e) With what banks do they work?
(Give exact particulars in case we wish to enquire about them.)
f) Do they live a long time in their present place?
g) Or in case they do not where did they live formerly?
h) Who is the head of the business—who is running it?
i) In case the partners are not running it, what is known of the men who are running it?

If Owned By a Corporation

6.

a) How do the shares stand?
b) What position (social, etc.) do the subscribers occupy?
c) Name some of the most respected by name and place of business.
d) Who is at the head?
e) What is known about their business contract?
f) Who runs the business and what is known about him?

7.

a) How long is the establishment the property of the present owners?
b) Who owned it formerly?
(If possible, state under what conditions it was sold, where the former owners now are and what they are doing now.)

8.

a) Is it known that the establishment already had suffered by fire?
b) Or that the owners had a fire with *other* property of theirs?
c) What was the damage in either, both instances?
d) What was the known or supposed origin of the fire?
e) Were the goods insured at the time and where were they insured?
f) Did the company continue the insurance after the fire?

Lodge Rooms over Moving Picture Incendiary Fire, 408-410 East 116th Street, Manhattan. "X" Marks Show Positions of Oil-Filled Bladders. Sixteen of these Bladders Found Unexploded.

9.

a) Where was the establishment insured up to now?
b) Since when?
c) Until when?
d) In what amounts?
e) At what premium annually?
f) Why does the insurance stop?
g) Was it offered lately to another company and was it refused?

10.

a) What risks does the owner have outstanding besides the one asked for? (Under this head belong all objects in the establishment on which insurance is not asked for.)
b) Where are they insured?
c) For what amount is each object insured and what premium is paid?
d) When do the policies run out on each item?

11.

a) Are the furnishings (especially machines) and fittings of old or modern construction?
b) In the latter case from what factory were they bought?
c) What system do they belong to (if there is one for them)?

12.

Are there any other features known which could help to judge the risk to be taken and which could influence the latter?

13.

Do you believe, leaving out all consideration of friendship and personal interest, in fullest sincerity and positive assurance that the company would take a desirable business by accepting this insurance?

14.

a) Do you know the parties *personally?*
b) Do you consider them absolutely moral and honest?
c) Have you *seen* the establishment and inspected it?
d) Did you find cleanliness in the shops and courts?
e) Do the buildings possess an exterior that points to orderliness, or do they look neglected?

15.

What other sources of information did you obtain?

16.

a) What premium do you consider should be demanded?
b) What premium did you mention to the parties?
c) What premium do you think he might accept?

Signature of the Agent.

....

APPENDIX "B"

Selections from

CORRESPONDENCE BETWEEN NEW YORK FIRE DEPARTMENT AND FOREIGN INSURANCE COMPANIES AS TO METHODS OF DEALING WITH APPLICATIONS FOR INSURANCE

During the course of the Fire Department Investigation into Incendiarism, a number of letters seeking information as to Foreign Fire Insurance methods were written to Foreign Insurance Companies; and a Circular embodying 12 Questions for them to answer was also sent out. Answers were received from 16 Foreign Fire Insurance Companies, whose names will be found on page 105 of this Report.

In the following pages, Replies to the Questions as given by 10 of the Companies are printed. The remaining answers are not given owing to having been similar in character to those printed.

Following the Answers to Questions will be found some of the "Proposal Forms" which English Companies require to be filled out by Applicants for Fire Insurance before Policies are issued.

ANSWERS TO QUESTIONS ASKED THE NORTH BRITISH AND MERCANTILE INSURANCE COMPANY OF LONDON (REPLY RECEIVED OCTOBER 1, 1912)

1. Q. On receipt of an application by the Company or its Agent for insurance on furniture or household effects, what steps, if any, does your Company or Agent take to ascertain the exact nature of the risk; and what inquiry, if any, is made as to the character or standing of the applicant?

A. Our agents or the Company's officials inspect the risks and satisfy themselves with regard to the position and standing of the applicant.

2, Q. Is it your custom to make any previous personal inspection of premises where small amounts of insurance on household effects are app ied for; and what form of report is made in such cases by the Company's representative (please send copy of form)?

A. Our agents or officials report on any special :eatures in the physical or moral risk. No fixed form of report in u e.

3. Q. Do you issue policies without previous inspection of property?

A. Yes, when the circumstances do not call for inspection.

4. Q. Is your business done through Agents, or directly with assured? If the latter, what is the nature of the questions put to applicant before issuing policy? (Please send application forms, if any.)

A. Through Agents, proposal form enclosed.

5. Q. If dealing through brokers, or agents, must these be licensed, or must they supply bonds; and if so, in how much; and what fees are paid?

A. No, in reply to both questions.

6. Q. Who issues the license to the brokers or agents; and for what cause or causes may those licenses be revoked, or the bond forfeited?

7. Q. In cases where fires occur, what is the method of your procedure to ascertain whether or not the fire is of suspicious origin or not?

A. As a general rule an independent assessor is employed to adjust and settle claims.

8. Q. In paying losses after fires, what steps do you take, if any, to prevent fraud, or the collection of insurance through fraudulent methods?

A. Depend upon circumstances, see answer to previous question.

9. Q. What steps, if any, are taken by your company to prevent or forestall the commission of arson with a view to the collection of insurance money?

Iron Works at 332 East 48th Street, in which an Elaborate "Fire Bug Plant" was Discovered. Building Burned was between Two Tenements, Fire Occurred About 1 A.M. Note Crowded Tenements on Either Side.

"Plant" Found Burning under Stairway at 332 East 48th Street. Note Candles in Box with Excelsior Piled Around.

A. The strict administration of the law of the country which imposes severe penalties on incendiaries is the main prevention.

10. Q. Have you any central bureau utilized by all companies, where suspicious fires are reported, and where records are kept of persons who have had previous fires?

A. No.

11. Q. What specified steps does your company take to protect itself in advance against fraudulent claims by means of arson?

A. See reply to Query 7.

12. Q. What steps does your company take, if any, to prevent applicants from over-insuring with your company?

A. See replies to Queries 1 and 2.

NORTH BRITISH AND MERCANTILE INSURANCE COMPANY.

ALLIANCE ASSURANCE COMPANY, LIMITED, BARTHOLOMEW LANE

LONDON, E. C., September 4, 1912.

NOTE—For questions see previous matter.

WILLIAM GUERIN, Esq., Acting Chief, Bureau of Fire Prevention, New York City:

Dear Sir—I am favored with your letter of the 28th ultimo and I have pleasure to reply to your queries in numerical order.

(1) We generally find that all the information we require in order to deal with simple risks and with household effects is furnished in the Proposal Forms (referred to in answer to No. 4), which have to be filled up and lodged with the office.

Special risks are usually inspected and reported upon by one of the Company's Surveyors.

(2) No, unless the information contained in the Proposal Form is insufficient or unsatisfactory.

(3) Yes, in connection with the great bulk of the business.

(4) Our business is done largely through Agents, who fill up the form marked "A," annexed, which has afterward to be sent to the Office. Where the business is direct and not through Agents we require the form marked "B" filled up, which has also to be sent to the Office.

(5) Insurance Brokers and Agents are not licensed, and it is seldom that we require a bond from a Broker or an Agent.

(6) See answer to No. 5.

(7) Losses are investigated by Assessors appointed by the Company. In some cases the Assessors are on the staff of the Office, but in most cases they are men who are not connected with any particular office and whose chief business is the assessing of losses for insurance companies.

(8) Losses are usually paid through the claimant's lawyers or through the Company's Agents, and the insured are communicated with direct from the Office before the losses are paid.

In many cases fires are notified in newspapers published in the district and are sent to the Office.

(9) No special steps are necessary.

(10) No.

(11) No special steps are necessary.

(12) None necessary.

I have the pleasure to enclose a copy of our standard Home Fire Insurance Policy.

Yours faithfully,

(Signed) R. LEWIS,
General Manager.

ANSWERS TO QUESTIONS ASKED THE PRUSSIAN NATIONAL INSURANCE COMPANY OF STETTIN, GERMANY

1. Q. On receipt of an application by the Company or its Agent for insurance on *furniture or household effects,* what steps, if any, does your Company or Agent take to ascertain the exact nature of the risk; and what inquiry, if any, is made as to the character or standing of the applicant?

A. Applications for insurance on *furniture and household effects* are usually made up by the Agents or other employees of the Company when *visiting the risk* offered. Though only trustworthy persons are appointed Agents, the latter do not make out the policy. This is done by the *general agency,* of which there is ordinarily only *one* in each Province of the Kingdom, after receipt of application, if the latter does not show cause for suspicion. Applications of doubtful nature are declined by the Company.

2. Q. Is it your custom to make any previous personal inspection of premises where small amounts of insurance on household effects are applied for; and what form of report is made in such cases by the Company's representative? (Please send copy of form.)

A. See answer under No. 1.

The enclosure No. 5 is required of Agent where it seems necessary to General Agency, unless already given previously.

3. Q. Do you issue policies without previous inspection of property?

A. See answer under No. 1.

4. Q. Is your business done through agents, or directly with assured? If the latter, what is the nature of the questions put to applicant before issuing policy? (Please send application forms, if any.)

A. Through Agents who sometimes have subagents. There are very few brokerage firms in Germany and these do no business in ordinary household risks.

5. Q. If dealing through brokers, or agents, must these be licensed, or must they supply bonds; and if so, in how much and what fees are paid?

A. No license, no bonds.

Only Provincial General Agents give securities to Company.

6. Q. Who issues the license to the brokers or agents; and for what cause or causes may those licenses be revoked or the bond forfeited?

7. Q. In cases where fires occur, what is the method of your procedure to ascertain whether or not the fire is of a suspicious origin or not?

A. Investigations as to the origin of the fire have generally already commenced at once and before the adjuster of the company arrives by the *fire department* and the *police.* If adjuster makes any discoveries pointing to arson he will at once inform the police of them; the Attorney General prosecuting arson where found out or suspected.

8. Q. In paying losses after fires, what steps do you take, if any, to prevent fraud, or the collection of insurance through fraudulent methods?

A. Company is not allowed to pay any claim on household furniture before previous advice to the police.

9. Q. What steps, if any, are taken by your company to prevent or forestall the commission of arson with a view to the collection of insurance money?

A. None.

10. Q. Have you any central bureau utilized by all companies, where suspicious fires are reported, and where records are kept of persons who have had previous fires?

A. No.

11. Q. What specified steps does your company take to protect itself in advance against fraudulent claims by means of arson?

A. See questions, etc., in enclosures Nos 3, 4 and 5 (forms for applications and Agents' reports).

12. Q. What steps does your company take, if any, to prevent applicants from over-insuring with your company?

A. Especially by careful selection of Agents.

PRUSSIAN NATIONAL INSURANCE COMPANY.

ANSWERS TO QUESTIONS ASKED THE NORTHERN ASSURANCE COMPANY LTD. OF LONDON, ENGLAND. (REPLY DATED SEPT. 12, 1912.)

NOTE—For questions see previous matter.

1. Unless well known to the Company or its Agent, the applicant is required to complete a Proposal Form. Specimen herewith.

2. No, but occasionally the circumstances are such that an inspection is deemed advisable, in which case a report is made by one of the Company's Surveyors.

3. Yes, speaking generally, policies applicable to private dwelling houses are issued without previous inspection of the property. In approved cases inspection is frequently dispensed with in other classes of risk, such, for instance, as Office Buildings, Non-Hazardous Shops and Farming Property. Policies are also usually issued without a further inspection in the case of property in Furniture Storing Warehouses and merchandise in Public Docks, Wharves and Warehouses, as these risks have been surveyed and the rates fixed.

4. Business is transacted both through Agents and directly with Insured. In the latter case a Proposal Form (as above) usually suffices for insurances applicable to

"Plant" Recently Found in Cellar at 332 East 48th Street, Manhattan.
Note Box with Candles, Excelsior Trailer.

private houses, offices and such like, but otherwise an inspection of the risk is made by one of the Company's Surveyors and inquiries may also be instituted as regards character and financial standing of applicant, when and if deemed desirable.

5 & 6. No license or bond is necessary so far as the transaction of fire insurance business is concerned.

7 & 8. Except in the case of quite small losses the matter is placed in the hands of a Fire Loss Assessor who reports thereon fully to the Company, and thereafter the agreed upon amount in settlement of the claim is exchanged for a form of discharge signed by the Insured. See also Condition XIII on specimen policy form herewith.

9. Unless an applicant for insurance is well known to the Company or its Agent, inquiries are made as to character and standing, with a view to preventing undesirable persons effecting insurances with the Company.

10. Certain of the larger cities here, such as London, Liverpool and Glasgow, maintain Salvage Corps, and from time to time suspicious cases are reported and the names of undesirables confidentially communicated to the Offices, but there is no central bureau where records are preserved of persons who have had previous fires.

11. See reply to Question No. 9.

Under our Policy Conditions all benefit under a Policy is forfeited in the event of the claim being a fraudulent one.

12. See reply to Question No. 9.

In cases where an inspection is made of the property the proposed amounts of insurance are usually in our possession before survey is made and in any other case, if there is reason to suspect over-insurance, the property would be inspected.

NORTHERN ASSURANCE CO. LTD.

ANSWERS TO QUESTIONS ASKED THE CENTURY INSURANCE COMPANY OF EDINBURGH, SCOTLAND. (RECD. SEPT. 30, 1912.)

1. Q. On receipt of an application by the Company or its Agent for insurance on furniture or household effects, what steps, if any, does your Company or Agent take to ascertain the exact nature of the risk; and what inquiry, if any, is made as to the character or standing of the applicant?

A. In almost every case of the kind the applicant is personally known to an Agent, representative or some person connected with the Office, and, therefore, we have at once a recommendation as to respectability. If situation too remote for inspection by an office official, the Agent can, as a rule, give particulars of the risk, but in most cases of ordinary private dwelling houses no inspection at all is necessary.

2. Q. Is it your custom to make any previous personal inspection of premises where small amounts of insurance on household effects are applied for; and what form of report is made in such cases by the Company's representative? (Please send copy of form.)

A. Reply to No. 1 also covers this.

3. Q. Do you issue policies without previous inspection of property?

A. Not in the case of any risk of importance. Probably only in such cases as are mentioned in queries Nos. 1 and 2.

4. Q. Is your business done through agents, or directly with assured? If the latter, what is the nature of the questions put to applicant before issuing policy? (Please send application forms, if any.)

A. Practically all through Agents. Copy of proposal form attached.

5. Q. If dealing through brokers, or agents, must these be licensed, or must they supply bonds; and if so, in how much and what fees are paid?

A. Agents do not require to be licensed in this country.

6. Q. Who issues the license to the brokers or agents; and for what cause or causes may those licenses be revoked or the bond forfeited?

7. Q. In cases where fires occur, what is the method of your procedure to ascertain whether or not the fire is of a suspicious origin or not?

A. All losses are carefully investigated by a competent Assessor, who ascertains all particulars connected with the loss and takes every possible step to protect the interests of the Company.

8. Q. In paying losses after fires, what steps do you take, if any, to prevent fraud, or the collection of insurance through fraudulent methods?

A. See reply to No. 7.

9. Q. What steps, if any, are taken by your company to prevent or forestall the commission of arson with a view to the collection of insurance money?

A. Make every possible inquiry as to thorough respectability and honesty of the Insured before issuing policy.

10. Q. Have you any central bureau utilized by all companies, where suspicious fires are reported, and where records are kept of persons who have had previous fires?

A. No recognized system of reporting suspicious fires, but any outstanding case would come to the knowledge of the Officials of the Associated Fire Offices, and particulars would be circulated.

11. Q. What specified steps does your company take to protect itself in advance against fraudulent claims by means of arson?

A. See reply to No. 9.

12. Q. What steps does your company take, if any, to prevent applicants from over-insuring with your company?

A. It is difficult to judge as to whether an applicant is over-insuring, but any obvious over-insurance would at once be noticed and questioned.

CENTURY INSURANCE CO. LTD.

ANSWERS TO QUESTIONS ASKED THE NORWICH UNION FIRE INSURANCE COMPANY, NORWICH, ENGLAND. (REPLY REC'D SEPT. 25, 1912, FROM J. F. VAN RIPER, BRANCH MANAGER, 59 JOHN STREET, NEW YORK CITY.)

1. Q. On receipt of an application by the Company or its Agent for insurance on furniture or household effects, what steps, if any, does your Company or Agent take to ascertain the exact nature of the risk; and what inquiry, if any, is made as to the character or standing of the applicant?

A. It is understood that the Agents satisfy themselves as to the bona fides of all persons to be insured for such risks.

2. Q. Is it your custom to make any previous personal inspection of premises where small amounts of insurance on household effects are applied for; and what form of report is made in such cases by the Company's representative? (Please send copy of form.)

A. No.

3. Q. Do you issue policies without previous inspection of property?

A. Yes, in a general way for simple risks, but inspections are made of all important industrial risks.

4. Q. Is your business done through agents, or directly with assured? If the latter, what is the nature of the questions put to applicant before issuing policy? (Please send application forms, if any.)

A. Sometimes one and sometimes the other, but much more frequently through Agents. Specimen of proposal form enclosed.

5. Q. If dealing through brokers, or agents, must these be licensed, or must they supply bonds; and if so, in how much and what fees are paid?

A. No. There are no such rules regarding Brokers, but Agents are sometimes required to furnish guarantee bonds.

6. Q. Who issues the license to the brokers or agents; and for what cause or causes may those licenses be revoked or the bond forfeited?

A. The guarantee bond for Agents can be forfeited in consequence of default in payment of premiums received or by any fraudulent act to the prejudice of the Office on the part of the Agent.

7. Q. In cases where fires occur, what is the method of your procedure to ascertain whether or not the fire is of a suspicious origin or not?

A. We rely upon the reports of our Agents and Assessors. Their procedure varies according to their views of the case.

8. Q. In paying losses after fires, what steps do you take, if any, to prevent fraud, or the collection of insurance through fraudulent methods?

A. Payment by crossed cheque in favor of assured passed through the hands of our Branch Manager or Agent.

9. Q. What steps, if any, are taken by your company to prevent or forestall the commission of arson with a view to the collection of insurance money?

A. Cases of arson are, in our experience, of very rare occurrence, which fact we believe to be due to the care exercised in the selection of business by our Branch Manager and Agents, who have in most instances a personal knowledge of the proposer.

10. Q. Have you any central bureau utilized by all companies, where suspicious fires are reported, and where records are kept of persons who have had previous fires?

A. No.

A Fire Bug Plant, the Most Elaborate of any ever found, was Uncovered at a Night Fire at 534 Vermont Street, Brooklyn, March 23, 1908. Openings in the Walls were Stuffed with Oakum, Connecting Trailers Leading to Oil-Soaked Clothing in Wardrobe. Interior of Building Draped and Festooned with Oakum, Leading to Gas Jets and Furniture. More than 2,000 Matches Found by Fire Marshal Brophy, who Caused Arrest of Occupants, Morris Weintraub and Nathan Weismann, who are now Fugitives from Justice. They Left Country, Forfeiting $10,000 Bail, which Amount was Added to City Treasury.

11. Q. What specified steps does your company take to protect itself in advance against fraudulent claims by means of arson?

A. See question 9.

12. Q. What steps does your company take, if any, to prevent applicants from over-insuring with your company?

A. In important cases the matter is dealt with by our Surveyors. In small cases we rely upon our Branch Managers and Agents.

Telegraphic Address: "Atlas, London."

ATLAS ASSURANCE COMPANY LIMITED, 92 CHEAPSIDE.

General Manager and Secretary, SAMUEL J. PIPKIN.

London, E. C., October 5, 1912.

Note—For questions see previous matter.

THE ACTING CHIEF,
Bureau of Fire Prevention,
Fire Department of The City of New York.

DEAR SIR—We are in receipt of your circular letter of August 28 and have pleasure in replying to your inquiries in respect of business in this country as follows:

1. Unless the amount is large, we do not deem it necessary, as a rule, in the case of simple proposals for the insurance of furniture and household effects, to make a survey to ascertain the physical nature of the risk. The standing and character of the applicant is a matter on which we satisfy ourselves by inquiry of a reference given by the applicant or by the Agent's statement that he is satisfied on the point.

2. This question is covered by our reply to No. 1. No special form of report used even when survey made.

3. Your inquiry as to whether policies are issued without previous inspection of property is not, we observe, limited to dwellings only. In the case of warehouse risks and risks of industrial or manufacturing character, surveys are in nearly every case made by a member of our specially trained survey department, unless the risk is already well known.

4. Our business is done both through Agents and direct, and we send you herewith copies of various proposal forms. There are comparatively few Agents who restrict themselves to fire insurance business.

5 & 6. Brokers and Agents in this country are not licensed.

7 & 8. It is only in the case of quite small losses that a settlement is taken in hand by our own Officials or Agents. Generally the adjustment of losses is undertaken by professional assessors, who from long experience are qualified in making searching inquiries as to the cause and suspicious origin or otherwise of the fire or possible fraud.

9. No special steps for the prevention or forestalling of arson are taken by the Company, apart from inquiry as to the character of the Insured and warning in the policy conditions that arson voids the insurance.

10. The answer is no, except to a limited extent, but Companies freely exchange information which is often the means of learning who are undesirable applicants.

11. Our answer to this question has been included in our comments above.

12. Our safeguard against over-insurance consists in the information we obtain as to the bona fide of the applicant, and our surveying officials in the case of large insurances have good opportunities of judging as to the amount of insurance proposed. Valuation prior to insurance, in order to circumvent the criminally inclined minority, would necessitate a heavy increase in the rates, which would be seriously prejudicial to the majority of the Insured.

Yours faithfully,

Manager.

ANSWERS TO QUESTIONS ASKED THE BRITISH AMERICA ASSURANCE COMPANY, TORONTO, CANADA. (REPLY DATED SEPT. 13, 1912.)

1. Q. On receipt of an application by the Company or its Agent for insurance on furniture or household effects, what steps, if any, does your Company or Agent take to ascertain the exact nature of the risk; and what inquiry, if any, is made as to the character or standing of the applicant?

A. Nearly all such applications come through Agents, and it is their duty to inspect and learn the exact nature of every risk they send in, including the character and standing of the applicant.

2. Q. Is it your custom to make any previous personal inspection of premises where small amounts of insurance on household effects are applied for; and what

form of report is made in such cases by the Company's representative? (Please send copy of form.)

A. The Agent is expected to make personal inspection whether amounts involved are large or small. No special form of report is called for.

3. Q. Do you issue policies without previous inspection of property?

A. No. With rare exceptions, which are listed for early inspection.

4. Q. Is your business done through agents, or directly with assured? If the latter, what is the nature of the questions put to applicant before issuing policy? (Please send application forms, if any.)

A. Chiefly through Agents. When directly with assured, all particulars considered necessary by the Management would be obtained through an Agent or employee of the Company.

5. Q. If dealing through brokers, or agents, must these be licensed, or must they supply bonds; and if so, in how much; and what fees are paid?

A. In some places Brokers and Agents are licensed by the municipality in which they operate. In many cases they give bonds to the companies they represent to secure the premiums collected by them. License fees vary in amount; bonds likewise.

6. Q. Who issues the license to the brokers or agents; and for what cause or causes may these licenses be revoked or the bond forfeited?

A. See answer to No. 5.

7. Q. In cases where fires occur, what is the method of your procedure to ascertain whether or not the fire is of suspicious origin or not?

A. Our Adjuster visits the scene of the fire and carefully investigates the physical evidences of the origin of the fire, interviewing also the assured and any witnesses available. The assured must also give a satisfactory account of his movements preceding the outbreak; in fact, the Adjuster must make a thorough investigation of every circumstance in connection with the loss.

8. Q. In paying losses after fires, what steps do you take, if any, to prevent fraud or the collection of insurance through fraudulent methods?

A. See answer to No. 7. This work is all covered by the Adjuster in handling the loss. If it is to be discovered at all, a fraudulent claim will almost always be detected before it is placed before the Company for payment.

9. Q. What steps, if any, are taken by your company to prevent or forestall the commission of arson with a view to the collection of insurance money?

A. The greatest protection is to see that the amount of insurance is kept within the actual value of the property, so that a margin of the value may be left as a responsibility upon the assured. This has the effect of encouraging the care rather than the destruction of the property. If there is reasonable suspicion of an intention to commit arson, the Company may relieve itself of liability by cancelling its policy.

10. Q. Have you any central bureau utilized by all companies, where suspicious fires are reported and where records are kept of persons who have had previous fires?

A. Yes. Underwriters Protective Association, 100 William street, New York.

11. Q. What specified steps does your company take to protect itself in advance against fraudulent claims by means of arson?

A. Action can only be taken when suspicion is aroused and company warned, when policy can be cancelled or other steps taken to defeat an attempt at arson. See also answer to No. 9.

12. Q. What steps does your company take, if any, to prevent applicants from over-insuring with your company?

A. The character of applicant and the value of property seeking insurance are the first things to be considered and a company in one way or another gets what it considers satisfactory evidence on these points before accepting the risk. Inspection by Agents and Company's officials are the chief means of protection against over-insurance.

BRITISH AMERICA ASSURANCE COMPANY.

Assistant General Manager.

Toronto, Canada, September 13, 1912.

ANSWERS TO QUESTIONS ASKED THE SCOTTISH UNION & NATIONAL INSURANCE COMPANY, EDINBURGH, SCOTLAND

1. Q. On receipt of an application by the Company or its Agent for insurance on furniture or household effects, what steps, if any, does your Company or Agent take to ascertain the exact nature of the risk; and what inquiry, if any, is made as to the character or standing of the applicant?

"Plant" in Sideboard at 534 Vermont Street, Brooklyn, Discovered March 23, 1908. Note Candle on Papers. The Fire Bugs, Morris Weintraub and Nathan Weismann, who are now Fugitives from Justice, Forfeited $10,000 Bail.

A. None, except that we rely on our Agents to forward applications only from persons known to them as of satisfactory character.

2. Q. Is it your custom to make any previous personal inspection of premises where small amounts of insurance on household effects are applied for; and what form of report is made in such cases by the Company's representative? (Please send copy of form.)

A. Not in connection with premises solely occupied as dwelling-houses.

3. Q. Do you issue policies without previous inspection of property?

A. Yes, for dwelling-houses and for certain other risks of an entirely non-hazardous character, also for certain storage warehouses, where we have information as to the risk satisfactory to us.

4. Q. Is your business done through agents, or directly with assured? If the latter, what is the nature of the questions put to applicant before issuing policy? (Please send application forms, if any.)

A. Both directly with the public and through Agents. We enclose copy of our form of proposal, showing the questions to be answered by the Agent.

5. Q. If dealing through brokers, or agents, must these be licensed, or must they supply bonds; and if so, in how much; and what fees are paid?

A. No. Brokers in this country are practically the same as Agents, and both receive the same allowance in the form of a commission on the premium.

6. Q. Who issues the license to the brokers or agents; and for what cause or causes may these licenses be revoked or the bond forfeited?

A. There are no licenses issued. The Company receives a form of application and appoints parties as its Agents during the pleasure of the Directors.

7. Q. In cases where fires occur, what is the method of your procedure to ascertain whether or not the fire is of suspicious origin or not?

A. In all fires of any size we employ a trained Fire Loss Assessor, part of whose duty it is to inquire into and report on the cause of the fire, and should there be any suspicious circumstances, these are always thoroughly investigated by him.

8. Q. In paying losses after fires, what steps do you take, if any, to prevent fraud or the collection of insurance through fraudulent methods?

A. We are protected by a condition in our policies, which voids the insurance if any claim be in any respect fraudulent.

9. Q. What steps, if any, are taken by your company to prevent or forestall the commission of arson with a view to the collection of insurance money?

A. We are protected by a condition in our policies, which voids the insurance if loss or damage be occasioned by or through the wilful act or procurement or connivance of the claimant.

10. Q. Have you any central bureau utilized by all companies, where suspicious fires are reported and where records are kept of persons who have had previous fires?

A. No. but the Companies endeavor as far as possible to communicate to each other the names of persons who are notorious claim makers or have had very suspicious fires.

11. Q. What specified steps does your company take to protect itself in advance against fraudulent claims by means of arson?

A. The only steps open to us to take are those of inspecting the property proposed to be insured, and satisfying ourselves as to the position and reputation of the applicant for insurance.

12. Q. What steps does your company take, if any, to prevent applicants from over-insuring with your company?

A. Generally the only opportunity of finding out such proposed over-insurance would be when the Company's Surveyor inspected the property.

Valued policies are not issued by the Company.

SCOTTISH UNION & NATIONAL INS. CO.

ANSWERS TO QUESTIONS ASKED THE ROYAL EXCHANGE ASSURANCE CORPORATION, LONDON, ENGLAND. (REPLY DATED SEPT. 5, 1912.)

1. Q. On receipt of an application by the Company or its Agent for insurance on furniture or household effects, what steps, if any, does your Company or Agent take to ascertain the exact nature of the risk; and what inquiry, if any, is made as to the character or standing of the applicant?

A. The Agent is supposed to know or to inquire regarding each applicant. The Company would in case of doubt ask the proposer for references. In shop and trade risks the place is inspected before acceptance; also, factory risks. Character of the proposer is found to be as important or more important than the nature of his shop or store.

2. Q. Is it your custom to make any previous personal inspection of premises where small amounts of insurance on household effects are applied for; and what form of report is made in such cases by the Company's representative? (Please send copy of form.)

A. The answer is in the negative. In small cases the proposer fills in a proposal form. Sample enclosed.

3. Q. Do you issue policies without previous inspection of property?

A. In the case of private houses almost invariably, and in other cases unless we consider the property requires inspection.

4. Q. Is your business done through agents, or directly with assured? If the latter, what is the nature of the questions put to applicant before issuing policy? (Please send application forms, if any.)

A. Through both sources. In the latter case one of the proposal forms is required to be filled up by the proposer.

5. Q. If dealing through brokers, or agents, must these be licensed, or must they supply bonds; and if so, in how much; and what fees are paid?

A. Brokers or Agents are not required to be licensed by any public authority. They do not as a rule furnish any bond. No fees are paid by them.

6. Q. Who issues the license to the brokers or agents; and for what cause or causes may these licenses be revoked or the bond forfeited?

A. There is no license. Each Company gives a letter of appointment or warrant to its Agent, and this is revocable at any time.

7. Q. In cases where fires occur, what is the method of your procedure to ascertain whether or not the fire is of suspicious origin or not?

A. We send an independent professional adjuster. These adjusters are in business as such on their own account, and most of them have acquired great experience through acting for many companies.

8. Q. In paying losses after fires, what steps do you take, if any, to prevent fraud or the collection of insurance through fraudulent methods?

A. See answer to No. 7.

9. Q. What steps, if any, are taken by your company to prevent or forestall the commission of arson with a view to the collection of insurance money?

A. By inspecting shop and trade risks before acceptance, and noting appearances and, if necessary, making private inquiries.

10. Q. Have you any central bureau utilized by all companies, where suspicious fires are reported and where records are kept of persons who have had previous fires?

A. The London Salvage Corps (maintained by the companies) keep such a record principally as regards London. Otherwise there is no central bureau, and companies keep their own records, if any.

11. Q. What specified steps does your company take to protect itself in advance against fraudulent claims by means of arson?

A. See answer to No. 9.

12. Q. What steps does your company take, if any, to prevent applicants from over-insuring with your company?

A. In trade risks our Inspector roughly checks the amount proposed from cursory inspection, and if the property is palpably over-insured we would decline the risk. In private houses under-insurance is the rule rather than the exception.

ROYAL EXCHANGE ASSURANCE CORPORATION.

E. M. Hiles.

London, England, Sept. 5, 1912.

"Plant" Showing Bottle Filled with Kerosene and "Trailer" Leading from Shelf under Dresser in Kitchen. This Fire Occurred at 534 Vermont Street, Brooklyn, March 23, 1908. The Fire Bugs, Morris Weintraub and Nathan Weismann—Now Fugitives from Justice—Forfeited Their Bail for $10,000.

............AGENCY. FIRE PROPOSAL.

ROYAL EXCHANGE ASSURANCE.

Head Office—Royal Exchange, London, E. C. 151A

West End Branch—44, Pall Mall, S. W.

Name of Proposer..
Address ....
Business or Profession..

QUESTIONS TO BE ANSWERED BY THE PROPOSER, AND WHICH WILL FORM PART OF THE BASIS OF THE PROPOSED INSURANCE.

1. Are you at present insured in this or any other Office? If so, please state particulars.
2. If not at present insured, where has the property been insured before, and to what amount?
3. Have you proposed to any Office and been refused?
4. **Have you ever had a fire, either in these premises or elsewhere? If so, state particulars.**
5. What trade (if any) is carried on in the adjoining premises?
6. By whom introduced.

Agent........................ *Signature of the Proposer*..........................

Address.................................... *Date*...................... 191...

QUESTIONS TO BE ANSWERED BY THE AGENT.

1. Are you personally acquainted with the Proposer?
2. Is the proposal one that you feel fully justified in recommending the Corporation to accept?
3. Do you consider the amounts proposed a fair insurable value for the property?
4. Are there any special features in the risk such as Stoves, Machinery, Hazardous Processes carried on, or Hazardous Goods stored?

Dated..................191 . *Agent's Signature*............................

ALLIANCE ASSURANCE COMPANY, LIMITED.

Head Office—Bartholomew Lane, London, E. C.

Established 1824.

PROPOSAL FOR FIRE INSURANCE.

QUESTIONS TO BE ANSWERED BY THE PROPOSER.

Name in full of Person to be insured.
Residence.
Occupation.
How long have you been in business in your present premises?
By whom recommended?
Are you already or have you been previously insured, and, if so, in what Office?
Has the risk been declined, and, if so, by what Office?
Have you had a loss by fire, and if so, when?

On building of
built of and roofed with
situate
On Twelve Months' Rent of said House

Sum To Be Insured.
£

On Household Goods, including Provisions, Stores, Wines and Liquors, Linen, Wearing Apparel, Cycles, Sporting Effects, Tenant's Fixtures and Fittings, Furniture, Carpets, Curtains, Printed Books and Printed Music, Plate and Cutlery..
On China, Earthenware, Glass, Looking Glasses, Musical and Scientific Instruments, Curiosities, Medals, Jewels, Trinkets, Clocks and Watches.
On Works of Art, including Pictures, Prints, Drawings, Sculpture, and Tapestry, no Work of Art, in case of Loss or Damage, to be valued at more than 5 per cent. of the amount insured under this item of the Policy ....
The property of the Insured and of his Servants, while contained in said Dwelling House.
On Stock and Utensils in Trade......................................
On Fixtures in Trade and Fittings up (*exclusive of Plate Glass and Plate Glass Fronts*) ....
On Plate Glass and Plate Glass Fronts............................
On Goods in Trust or on Commission..............................
On Horses, Harness, Carriages, Stable Utensils, and Fodder in situate ....

.....................191 Total ....£

Signature of Proposer................................

NORTH BRITISH & MERCANTILE INSURANCE COMPANY.

Established 1809.

In Which Are Vested the Shares of
The Ocean Marine Insurance Company, Limited.
The Railway Passengers Assurance Company.
61 Threadneedle Street, London, E. C.

Total Funds............£21,250,000. Annual Income............£5,000,000.

PROPOSAL FOR FIRE INSURANCE.

Proposer's Name in full...
Residence ....
Rank, Profession, or Trade..

Property To Be Insured.

Sum To Be Insured.

1. On Building situate..
   built of.......................roofed with....................
   occupied as ....£
   (If a trade be carried on state whether sale shop or if there be any process of manufacture.)
2. On One Year's Rent of the same................................£
3. On Household Furniture and effects...........................£
   (Not more than £ on any one Painting, Engraving, Print, Drawing, or piece of Sculpture.)
4. On Trade Fixtures and Fittings (Plate Glass Shop Front excepted) ....£
5. On Plate Glass Shop Front......................................£
6. On Stock and Utensils in Trade................................£
7. On Goods in Trust or on Commission, for which Proposer is responsible ....£
8. On Building of Stable and Coach-house situate....................
   ....built of...........................
   roofed with ....£
9. On Horses, Harness, Carriages, Stable Utensils and Fodder therein.£
10. On other Property as per particulars below:

Total ....£

QUESTIONS TO BE ANSWERED BY PROPOSER AND WHICH WILL FORM PART OF THE BASIS OF THE INSURANCE.

How long have you occupied these premises?
If not wholly in your own occupation, state particulars?
Have you ever made a claim for Loss by Fire either at the above or any other premises?
Has the Insurance been offered to any other Office?
Has any proposal for Fire Insurance made by you or on your behalf ever been declined by this or any other Insurance Company?
Is this proposal in lieu of, or in addition to, any former Insurance in this Office?
On whose recommendation do you make this proposal?

Signature of Agent.................... *Signature of Proposer*...................
Date.................................

(Subject to the Conditions of Insurance as printed on the Company's Policies.)

THE YORKSHIRE INSURANCE COMPANY, LTD.

PROPOSAL FORM.

Excluding Pawnbrokers

Christian and Surname in full..
Residence ....
Profession or Business..

No.	Property to be Insured.	Sums to be Insured.	Rate.
1.	On the Building of the *Dwellinghouse and Shop* communicating and Domestic Out offices adjoining thereto. Built of Brick, Stone, Tile, or Slate, situate No..............	£	
2.	On Household Furniture and Effects (£10 limit on any one Print or Picture) in private use only, therein............	£	
3.	On Stock-in-Trade and movable utensils therein............	£	
4.	On Trade Fixtures and Fittings (exclusive of Plate-glass and Plate-glass Fronts) therein........................	£	
5.	On Plate-glass and Plate-glass Fronts therein..............	£	
6.	On Goods in trust or on Commission, for which the Proposer is responsible, therein................................	£	
7.	On the Building of the *Warehouse*, built of Brick, Stone, Tile, or Slate, situate..................................	£	
8.	On Stock and Utensils in Trade, Fixtures and Fittings, therein	£	
9.	On the Building of the *Coach-house and Stable* adjoining each other, built of Brick, Stone, Tile, or Slate, situate..	£	
10.	On Horses (£40 limit on any one animal), Harness, Vehicles, Stable Utensils, and Fodder, therein....................	£	
11.	On 12 Months' *Rent*	£	
		£	

Buildings *standing alone*, or *separated* from adjoining Buildings by a *Party Wall*, must have a *separate* sum upon each, also a *separate* sum for the property *contained* in each.

PLEASE STATE:

1. Are the premises occupied solely by the Proposer? If not, please say how otherwise tenanted?

2. How many Assistants (*i. e.*, all hands working on the premises, except outside Messengers, Porters and Domestic Servants) are employed on the premises?

3. Are the premises heated otherwise than by Common Fireplaces, or Gas Stoves standing on stone flags or fire tiles, and having metal pipes only?

If so, describe arrangements.

If by Stove, state on what material it stands, length of pipe, and how vented and protected?

4. Are the premises lighted otherwise than by Ordinary Coal Gas?

If the proposal relates to the premises of (*A*) *a Grocer, Italian Warehouseman, Tea or Provision Dealer, Ironmonger, Dealer in Lamps, Paints, Oils and Colors, Ship Chandler, or Chemist and Druggist*—

5. Are any inflammable goods kept, such as Gunpowder, Turpentine, Naphtha, Mineral Oil, or its products, or Matches?

If so, state the quantities of each, and where stored.

In the case of Mineral Oil, is an inflammable vapor under 73 degrees Fahr. given off?

6. Is any manufacturing process carried on, such as roasting Coffee or Chicory, grinding by or use of power of any kind, smoking provisions or any process by artificial heat?

Or (*B*) *Draper, Haberdasher, Costumer, Milliner, Mantlemaker, Dressmaker, Hosier, Furniture Dealer, or Upholsterer*—

7. Are the display windows lighted from the outside or inside?

8. Are the lights in Shop and Windows protected by Globes?

N. B.—It must be warranted that no goods be hung over or within 12 inches of lights.

Does this proposal cancel a previous Policy?
If so, quote the number...........

(*Continued next page.*)

THE FOLLOWING QUESTIONS TO BE ANSWERED BY THE AGENT.

1. Is the Proposer well known to you, and are you satisfied as to his character and commercial standing?
2. How long has the business been conducted by Proposer in these premises?
3. How long has he carried on the same business in any former premises, and where?
4. **Has a fire occurred in any premises occupied by the Proposer, if so, state particulars?**
5. Are the premises separated from adjoining risks by a complete brick or stone party wall, without opening of any kind therein?
6. How are the adjoining buildings constructed and occupied?
7. Are the adjoining buildings or contents insured in this Office?
8. Has the Proposer any Insurances on this or other property current with this Company?
9. Is there any existing Insurance with any other Company on the property now proposed?
10. Has the Proposer ever been declined by any Office?
11. Is there any special feature connected with the risk proposed, and are there any further remarks which occur to you, and important for the Company to know?

Agency................................

................................191

I have pleasure in submitting the within proposal, and above are my replies to the usual questions.

(Signed) ....

Agent.

N. B.—In all cases where there are several buildings, a rough ground sketch will be of material assistance.

THE NORTHERN ASSURANCE COMPANY LTD.

FORM OF PROPOSAL FOR FIRE INSURANCE.

.......................19

Full Name and Address of the Person in whose favor the Insurance is to be effected ....

NOTE—IF THERE IS A SHOP IN THE BUILDING PLEASE GIVE PARTICULARS OF PROPOSAL OVER LEAF.

£ On *Household Furniture and other Personal Effects* in the *Dwelling House and Offices* communicating therewith, situate
built of and covered with
The amount which can be recovered on any one Picture, Print, Drawing, Sculpture, or other Work of Art, or any one Medal or other Curiosity, under above item will be fixed relatively to the sum insured.

£ On the Building of said *Dwelling House and Offices.*

£ On *Twelve Months' Rent of said House.*
Please state whether payable or receivable.

£ On the Building of the *Coach House and Stable* (communicating with each other or under one roof), situate near the aforesaid Dwelling House (*if otherwise, please state the situation*), built of
and covered with

£ On *Horses, Vehicles, Harness, Stable Utensils and Fodder therein.*
If the Coach House and Stables are distinct Buildings, separate sums are necessary for the Buildings and Contents of each respectively.

£

N. B.—If there is other property to be insured please describe same, giving separate sum for each distinct building and its contents.

£ On the BUILDING of house having a Shop therein
situate
built of and covered with

£ On Stock and Utensils in Trade.

£ On Goods in Trust or on Commission, *for which Insured is responsible.*

£ On Fixtures (*exclusive of Plate Glass and Plate Glass Fronts*).

£ On Plate Glass Fronts and Mirrors being Fixtures in Trade.

£ On Household Furniture, Linen, Wearing Apparel, Printed Books, Plate, Wine and other Liquors in private use.

£ On Watches, Clocks, Jewels and Trinkets.

£ On Philosophical and Musical Instruments and Printed Music.

£ On Pictures, Prints and Drawings (limit on any one, £5).

£ On China and Glass, Earthenware and Looking Glasses.

(These Items may be included in one if desired.)

£ On Twelve Months' Rent of said House and Shop.
Please state whether payable or receivable.

£

N. B.—If any Stoves or Implements for producing Fire-heat other than Common Grates or Gas Stoves are used, or process of Manufacture carried on, these should be specially described.

If Mineral Oils sold, please state quality and quantity, and where kept.

QUESTIONS TO BE ANSWERED BY THE PROPOSER.

How long have you resided in the premises referred to?

Is the property proposed for Insurance already insured in this or any other Office? If so, where and for what amount?

Have you ever sustained any Loss by Fire?

Has any Insurance Company ever declined to insure your property, or that for which you are responsible, or refused to continue an existing insurance?

On whose recommendation have you applied to the "NORTHERN"? If not that of an Agent or client of the Company, please give name and address of a referee.

Signature of Proposer......................................

Agency................................ *Policy No*............

For Buildings and Contents of Private Dwelling-houses only. Town.

ATLAS ASSURANCE COMPANY, LIMITED,

Fire, Life, Accident & Burglary.

FIRE PROPOSAL.

Head Office—92 Cheapside, London, E. C.

Proposer's full name..
(If a Lady, please state whether Single, Married, or Widow.)

Address ....
Occupation ....

Sum To Be Insured.

1. On the Building occupied solely as a Private Dwelling-house and Domestic Offices, all communicating or under the same roof therewith, situate .... £
2. On the Buildings of the Stables, Coach-houses and Out-buildings, situate adjoining or near to the said Dwelling-house................ £
3. On Furniture, household and personal effects (limit on any one Curio, Picture or other Work of Art five per cent.) of the Insured, or of members of his family or of his servants, including such property up to ten per cent. of the sum insured (if not otherwise insured) whilst temporarily removed other than for the purpose of Sale or Exhibition to and contained in any other private Dwelling-house or any Lodging-house, Hotel, Club, Bank or Safe Deposit (not being part of a Furniture Depository) in the United Kingdom, all in private use .... £
4. On Horses, Harness, Carriages (Motor Vehicles excepted), Fodder, and Stable Utensils in said Stables, Coach-houses and Out-buildings .... £
5. On twelve months' Rent of the above Buildings in proportion to the respective amounts insured thereon........................... £
6. On .... £
7. On Boundary Walls, Gates, and Fences, belonging to the aforesaid Premises .... £

☞Specific sums are required upon the buildings and contents respectively of each separate building.

£

QUESTIONS TO BE ANSWERED BY PROPOSER.

1. Has any other Office declined to accept or continue your Insurance?
2. Have you ever made a claim against an Insurance Company? If so, please give particulars.
3. Is the property already insured? If so, give name of Office and amount.
4. Of what materials are the external walls and roofs constructed?
5. How are the premises lighted: by electricity, gas, or oil lamps?
6. **On whose recommendation do you make this proposal to the Atlas?**

Dated.......................... *Signature of Proposer*..........................

☞Information in reply to the foregoing questions will save much time in dealing with the proposal.

INDEX.

A

PAGE
Ackerley, Annie, fire bug 90-92
Adjusters, public 50
Chap. V, contract 51
Padding claims 51
Commissions 51-52
Brokers 52
Incendiaries 52
Swindling the assured 53
Robt. J. Lawrence on crooked 55
Agricultural Insurance Co., policy 35
Albany Insurance Co., policy 35
Alliance Assurance Co., of London, questions asked applicants 107, 131
Amonson, Louis S., opinion on insurance and arson 14
American Central Insurance Co., of St. Louis, policy 39
American Union Insurance Co., of Philadelphia, policy 39
American Fire Insurance Co., policy 36
American Insurance Co., of Newark, policies 31, 40
Areas, contrasts in fire, New York 16-21
Arson—Percentage of 13
Convictions for 56
Skill of incendiaries 56
"Trust" 59-60
Fishman case 63
Calandra 67
Difficulties of conviction 99
How to stop 100
Cases, Chapters VI., VII. and VIII. 68-99
Articles insured by Fire Department, list of, at 239 East 101st street 25
At 69 West 101st street 37
At 203 East 77th street 38
At 220 East 36th street 40
Atlas Assurance Co., of London, policy 35
Questions to applicants abroad 108
Answers to questions *re* foreign methods. 139
"Blacklist" of foreign applicants 108

B

Bainbridge, Jno. K., policy 41
Bainbridge & White, policy 42
Barr, Samuel, in Brant case 68
Benedict & Benedict, policy 31, 36, 42
Berlin—Fires in 1911 100
Fires per 100,000 population 100
Fire loss per capita 100
Bertolino, Antonio, case 46-47
Judge Swann on 47-48
Boston Insurance Co., policy 35
Bostwick, Chas. P., in Bertolino case 48
Board of Underwriters, New York, "previous fires" 108
Brant, Samuel, fire bug 68, 71
British American Assurance Co., of Toronto, answers to questions 105, 139-140
Brokers, licensed, total number in New York 101
Brokers and Fire Insurance Exchange 101
Brown, H. W., & Co., policy 35
Brown, T. Y., & Co., letter from, *re* Granite State policy 26
Policy 39, 40
Brown, Williard S., policy 39
Brown, W. S., & Co., policy 35, 39
Brophy, Thos. P., Fire Marshal—Estimate of arson 14, 100
In Brant case 68
In Greenberg horse-burning case 72, 75
In Annie Ackerley case 93
In Singer case 96
Brownstein, Benjamin, fire bug 68,71
Business fires, Chapter IV 44, 45, 46, 47
Buffalo German Insurance Co., policy 35

C

Capitol Insurance Co., of Concord, policy .. 39
California Insurance Co., of San Francisco, policy 35
Caledonian Insurance Co., policy 26, 31, 35
Calumet Insurance Co., of Chicago, policy .. 36
Calandra, Biagio, case 64, 67
Century Insurance Co. of Edinburgh—Binder 35
Answers to questions *re* foreign methods 107, 135-136
Central National Insurance Co., of Chicago, policy 36
Chicago "Arson Trust" 59-60, 63
Citizens Insurance Co., of Charlestown, W. Va., policy 35
Citizens Insurance Co., of Missouri policy .. 36
City of New York Insurance Co., policy 34
Cloaks and women's suit fires 44
Commercial Union Assurance Co. of London, policy 34, 35
In Annie Singer case 99
Commonwealth Insurance Co. of New York, policy 35
Companies, insurance, policies at 239 East 101st street, list 31
69 West 101st street, list 34-36
203 East 77th street, list 38-39
220 East 36th street, list 40-41
208 East 73d street, list 42
Commerce Insurance Co., of Albany, policy .. 39
Contents, table of 11
Concordia Insurance Co., of Milwaukee, policy 35
Connecticut Insurance Co., of Hartford, policies 35 (2), 39
Contrasts in fire areas, New York 16, 21
Continental Fire Insurance Co., policy 31
Correspondence, replies to Fire Department from foreign fire insurance companies 128-144
County Fire Insurance Co., of Philadelphia, policy 35
Cremins, M. J., policy 38, 39, 40
Crum & Forster, policy 35, 36, 38, 39, 41

D

Detroit Fire & Marine Insurance Co 36
De Malignon, Herman, Assistant Fire Marshal, in Steinkreutzer case 84-88
Delaware Insurance Co., of Philadelphia, policy 39
Dike, Judge Norman J.—In Galasso case .. 79
In Greenberg case 75
In Ackerley case 93
Dinsmore, Wm., & Son, policy 41
Dixie Fire Insurance Co., policy 41
Dodd, Magistrate, censure of Greenberg 72
Dreyfus, Leopold, Chicago fire bug case 60
Dubuque Fire & Marine Insurance Co., policy 40
Dutchess Fire Insurance Co 39
Duross Co., policy 39

E

Eaton, Henry W., replies to questions *re* foreign fire insurance methods, Liverpool & London & Globe Co 106
East 101st street apartment 25
Embroidery trade fires 44
Etna Fire Insurance Co., of Hartford, policy 42

PAGE
Equitable Fire & Marine Co., of Providence, policy ... 40
European fires, comparison with New York. 100
Evans, Louis, self-confessed fire bug, horse-burning case ... 72, 75

F

Farmers Insurance Co., of York, Pa., policy. 41
Feldman, Hy., & Son, policy ... 35
Fire Insurance Exchange and brokers' licenses ... 101
Fire Association of Philadelphia, policy ... 35
  In Annie Singer, fire bug, case ... 71
  In Tirnauer case ... 83
Fires, incendiary—In business and trades, Chapter IV. ... 43-49
  Berlin ... 100
  Cases, Chapters VI., VII. and VIII. ... 68-99
  Dresden ... 100
  Foreign ... 100
  Insurance ... 46
  In novelty and toy trade ... 44
  In shirtwaist trade ... 44-45
  In hat and cap trade ... 44-45
  In cloak and women's suits ... 44
  In leather goods ... 44
  In embroidery ... 44-45
  In millinery ... 44-45
  London ... 100
  New York City, 1911 ... 100
  Not ascertained ... 44
  Per 100,000 of population ... 100
  Per capita, compared to foreign cities ... 100
  Paris ... 100
  Suspicious ... 46
  St. Petersburg ... 100
  Southampton ... 100
  Vienna ... 100
Fire bugs cases:
  Ackerley, Annie ... 90-94
  Bertolino ... 46
  Brant ... 68-71
  Chicago Arson Trust ... 59-63
  Evans ... 72-75
  Fishman ... 63
  Galasso ... 76-77
  Greenberg ... 72-75
  Horowitz, Jacob ... 89-90
  Horse burners ... 72-76
  Michaels, Mattie ... 95
  Ostrinsky ... 95-99
  Paterson ... 89-90
  Singer, Annie ... 95-99
  Steinkreutzer, Isadore ... 84-88
  Tirnauer ... 77-78
  Wasserman ... 72-75
Fire insurance companies—Want fires ... 43
  Lists of policies. 31, 34, 35, 36, 38, 39, 40, 41, 42
Fireman's Insurance Co., of Newark, policy. 42
Fidelity Phoenix Insurance Co., of New York, policy ... 35, 40
Fireman's Fund Insurance Co., of San Francisco, policy ... 35
Fire Insurance Exchange—Cancellation of policies ... 30
  Brokers and ... 101
"Fire Bug District," New York ... 16, 17, 18, 19
Fire Department, summary of work done in obtaining insurance ... 15
  Account of obtaining insurance, Chapters II. and III. ... 25-42
Fire Marshals, estimates of fire loss, New York ... 13, 14
Fire loss—Estimate by Fire Marshals ... 13
  Foreign ... 100
  Per capita ... 100
  New York ... 100
"Flash fires" ... 94
Fishman, Morris, incendiary case ... 63
Flower and feather trade fires ... 44
Foreign fires ... 100
Foreign fire insurance companies, list of ... 105
Foreman & Herman, policy ... 31, 38, 42
Freund, V., & Son, policy ... 36
Fur trade fires ... 44

G

PAGE
Gaynor, Hon. Wm. J., Mayor, letter to, by Commissioner Johnson ... 5
Galasso, Andrea, case ... 76-79
German fire insurance companies, questions asked applicants ... 43
  See also Appendix A ... 115-127
Germania Insurance Co., policy ... 28
  Agent's inspection at East 101st street ... 28
  Policy ... 31
German-American Insurance Co. of Philadelphia, policy ... 41
German-American Insurance Co. of Baltimore, policy ... 35
German-American Insurance Company of New York, policy ... 35
German Fire Insurance Co. of Wheeling, policy ... 42
German Alliance Insurance Co., letter from, declining insurance ... 27
  Policy ... 35
Glens Falls Insurance Co., policy ... 36, 40
Gold, Samuel, in Steinkreutzer case ... 84, 87-88
Goodman, Wm., policy ... 31, 35
Granite State Insurance Co., policy ... 26-27
  List ... 31
Greenfeder, Joseph, in horse-burning case .. 75-76
Greenfeder, Isaac, stable fire ... 76
Greenberg, Morris and David ... 72, 75
Greenwich Insurance Co. of New York, policy ... 36
Guerin, Chief Wm.—"Insurable interest" .. 30
  Letter to, from Sun Insurance Office, London ... 109
  Letter to, from Alliance Assurance Co ... 131
  In Steinkreutzer case ... 84

H

Hall, E., & Co., policy ... 35
Hall & Henshaw, policy ... 35, 38, 39, 40
Hanover Insurance Co. of New York, policy. 34
Halpin, Fireman James, and Galasso case ... 76
Hat and cap fires, New York ... 44
Hamburg-Bremen Fire Insurance Co., policy. 36
Hartford Fire Insurance Co., policy ... 31, 39
Helbing, Julius W., policy ... 39
Herbertz & Miller, letter from, declining insurance ... 28
Herrick, H., policy ... 36
Hilliard, J. G., policy ... 34, 35, 38, 39, 40, 41, 42
Home Insurance Co., New York, policy ... 31
Horowitz, Jacob, fire bug, Paterson case ... 89
Horse burners ... 72, 75
Howe, Battalion Chief John, woman fire bug case ... 94
Howe, First Grade Fireman Washington—Insurance ... 25, 27, 28
  In Steinkreutzer case ... 84, 88

I

Imperial Fire Insurance Co. of Denver, policy ... 42
Incendiarism—As lucrative trade ... 5
  Trade fires, Chapter IV ... 43-49
  Fishman case ... 63
  Bertolino case ... 46
  Various cases, Chapters VI., VII. and VIII. ... 68, 99
  Limitation of insurance ... 21
Incendiaries, cases:
  Ackerley ... 90, 94
  Adjusters and ... 54
  "Arson Trust" ... 59-63
  Brant ... 68,71
  Evans ... 72, 75
  Finances and ... 60
  Galasso ... 76, 79
  Greenberg ... 72, 75
  Horowitz ... 89-90
  Horse burners ... 72, 75
  Michaels ... 95
  Ostrinsky ... 69
  Paterson cases ... 89-90
  Singer ... 95-99

PAGE

Incendiaries, cases:
- Skill of ... 56
- Steinkreutzer ... 84, 88
- Tirnauer ... 79, 80
- Trial and convictions ... 56
- Wasserman ... 72, 75

Incendiary Bands—Organized ... 21
- Fires by, Judge Swann on ... 49

Inspection by German companies abroad .. 120-127
Insurance, New York, worst district in ... 26
Insurance—Limitation of, as preventive of arson ... 21-22
- Obtaining 135 policies by New York Fire Department ... 25-42
- Total amount at risk ... 101
- Total loss by fires ... 101
- Capital invested ... 101

Insurance companies ... 22
- Policies at 239 East 101st street ... 29
- List ... 31
- At 69 West 101st street, list ... 34-36
- At 203 East 77th street ... 38-39
- At 220 East 36th street, list ... 40-41
- At 208 East 73d street ... 42
- Bertolino case ... 47, 49
- Number of New York ... 101
- Responsibility of ... 101
- Foreign, in New York ... 101
- German ... 101-102, 115-127
- List of foreign ... 105
- Correspondence with, see Appendix B. 128-144

"Insurable interest" ... 30
Insurance Co. of North America, policies .. 34-35
Insurance Co., State of Pennsylvania, policy 34

J

James, F. S., & Co., policy ... 31, 36, 40
Jillson, F. E., letter to Wade, *re* policy ... 32
- Policy ... 31, 39

Johnson, Joseph, Fire Commissioner, New York, letter of, to Mayor ... 5
- Judge Swann's letter to ... 49

Joerns & French, policy ... 31

K

Kelly & Fuller, policy ... 35, 38, 39

L

Lawrence, Robert J., of "Spectator," on crooked adjusters ... 55
Law Union & Rock Insurance Co. of London, policy ... 35
Leather goods, fires in trade ... 44
Legislative Joint Committee, *re* insurance agents ... 14
- Testimony before, by Stoddart ... 38

Limbach & Behning, policy ... 31
Liverpool & London & Globe Insurance Co., policies ... 26, 31
- Duplication of policies ... 32
- Policy list ... 31 (3)
- Answers to questions *re* foreign methods. 106

Lists of policies—At 239 East 101st street .. 31
- At 69 West 101st street ... 34-36
- At 203 East 77th street ... 38-39
- At 220 East 36th street ... 40-41
- At 208 East 73d street ... 42

List of foreign companies ... 105
Lockwood Bros., policy ... 35
London Assurance Corporation, policy ... 35
London & Lancashire Insurance Co.—Cancellation of policy ... 33
- List ... 31

London fires—In 1911 ... 100
- Per 100,000 population ... 100
- Per capita ... 100

Lumbermen's Insurance Co. of Philadelphia. 41
Lumber Insurance Co. of New York ... 39

M

Mainzer, Robert H.—Report on foreign fire insurance methods ... 101-103
- Translation of German proposal forms, see Appendix "A" ... 113-127

PAGE

Mechanics & Traders Insurance Co. of New Orleans, policy ... 39
Mechanics Insurance Co. of Philadelphia, policy ... 35
Merchants Fire Insurance Co. of Denver, policy ... 41
Michaels, Mattie, fire bug ... 95
Millinery trade fires ... 44
Millers National Insurance Co. of Chicago. 42
Mills, A. B., policy ... 35, 39, 40
Milwaukee Mechanics Insurance Co., policy. 39

N

National Ben Franklin Insurance Co., policy ... 25, 35
Nationale Insurance Co. of Paris, policy ... 39
National Union of Pittsburg, policy ... 31
National Insurance Co. of Hartford, policy .. 40
Nassau Insurance Co. of Brooklyn, policy .. 41
National Lumber Insurance Co. of Buffalo. 41
New Brunswick Fire Insurance Co., policy. 39
New Jersey Fire Insurance Co. of Newark, policy ... 39
Newman & McBain, policy ... 35, 39, 40, 41, 42
New York Board of Underwriters and "previous fires" ... 108
Newark Fire Insurance Co. of New Jersey ... 31, 36
Niagara Insurance Co. of New York, policy. 35
Northwestern National of Milwaukee, policy ... 31, 41
Northern Assurance Co. of London—Policy list ... 34
- Questions asked applicants abroad. 107, 132, 135
- Horse-burning case ... 72

North British & Mercantile, policy ... 39
- Answers to questions *re* foreign methods ... 128, 131

North River Insurance Co. policy ... 35
Northern Insurance Co. of New York, policy 39
Novelties and toy trade fires ... 44
Norwich Union Insurance Co. of England, policy ... 31
- Answer to questions *re* foreign methods ... 106, 136, 139

O

O'Brien & O'Brien, policy ... 35, 39
Ogden, W. B., & Son, policy ... 31, 36, 39
Orient Insurance Co. of Hartford, policy ... 35
Old Colony Insurance Co. of Boston, policy. 39
Ohio Farmers Insurance Co., policy ... 42
Ostrinsky, Jacob, fire bug ... 96

P

Paris fires—In 1911 ... 100
- Per 100,000 of population ... 100
- Loss per capita ... 100

Pacific Insurance Co. of New York, policy. 39
Palatine Insurance Co. of London, policy .. 35
Paterson incendiaries, Chief Stagg on .. 21, 89-90
Pearlman, Max, Paterson fire ... 89-90
Pelican Assurance Co. of New York ... 39
Pennsylvania Insurance Co. of Philadelphia, policy ... 39
People's National Insurance Co. of Philadelphia ... 41-42
Perrin, W. L., & Son, policy ... 40, 41, 42
Phoenix Assurance Co. of London, policy ... 35
- Policy conditions abroad ... 107

Phoenix Insurance Co. of Hartford, policy .. 39
Pittsburg Fire Insurance Co., policy ... 39
Policies—Total number ... 29
- Ease in obtaining ... 42
- Recapitulation ... 42
- Lists of, secured by Fire Department at 239 East 101st street ... 29
- List ... 31
- At 69 West 101st street, list ... 34, 35-36
- At 203 East 77th street ... 38-39
- At 220 East 36th street ... 40-41
- At 208 East 73d street ... 42

PAGE
Providence Washington Insurance Co., of Providence, policy ... 41
Prial, John P., Fire Marshal, Manhattan—Estimate of percentage of arson ... 14
In Steinkreutzer case ... 84, 87-88
In Fishman case ... 63
Providentia Insurance Co., Frankfurt, Germany—Questions asked applicants ... 104
See also Appendix "A" ... 115, 127
Proof of loss and fire bugs ... 41
Prussian National Insurance Co., of Stettin, Germany—Policy ... 5
Answers to questions *re* German methods ... 131-132
Public Adjusters—Chapter V., contract ... 53
Padding claims ... 51
Commissions ... 51-52
Brokers and ... 52
Incendiarism and ... 53
Swindling ... 54
Robert J. Lawrence, opinion on ... 55

Q

Queens Insurance Co., policy, list ... 34

R

Recommendations *re* insurance and incendiarism ... 111
Recapitulation of insurance policies ... 42
Reid, Wallace, policy ... 31, 35
Remedies, Chapter IX ... 100, 111
Rhode Island Insurance Co. of Providence .. 39
Reliance Insurance Co. of Philadelphia, policy ... 39
Ross, F. H.—Estimate of arson ... 13-14
Letter to Fire Commissioner Johnson on fire losses ... 29
On incendiarism ... 100
Policy ... 35
Royal Exchange Assurance Co. of London—Policy ... 31
Replies to questions *re* foreign methods. 143-144
Questions to applicants ... 107
Royal Insurance Co. of Liverpool, policy ... 35

S

Security Insurance Co. of New Haven, policy ... 38
Schell, R. D., & Son, policy ... 35
Schmidt & Donahue, policy ... 35
Scottish Union & National Insurance Co. of Edinburgh—Policies ... 34, 40
Questions to applicants abroad ... 107
Answers to questions *re* foreign methods ... 140, 143
Shirtwaist trade fires ... 44
Short & Co., policy ... 36
Singer, Mrs. Annie, fire bug ... 95-99
Smith, Chas. G., policy ... 38, 39
Sohmer, Wm., policy ... 35, 39
Springfield Fire & Marine Insurance Co., policy ... 38
St. Petersburg, fires in, per 100,000 population ... 100
Stuyvesant Insurance Co., policy ... 38
St. Paul Fire & Marine Insurance Co., policy ... 38
Stagg, John, Ex-Chief, Paterson Fire Department, on incendiary fires and insurance. 21
Standard Fire Insurance Co. of Hartford, policy ... 41

PAGE
Starkweather & Shepley, policy ... 31, 39
Steinkreutzer, Isadore, fire bug ... 84-88
Stoddart, John H., admissions before Joint Committee on hazardous risks ... 38
Stable fires ... 76
Suspicious fires ... 46
Sullivan, Fire Attorney, of Chicago, on "Arson Trust" ... 63
Sun Fire Insurance Co. of New Orleans—Policy ... 28
List ... 31
Questions to foreign applicants ... 108
Svea Insurance Co. of Gottenburg, Sweden, policy ... 40
Swann, Judge Edward—In Bertolino case ... 47
On incendiary fires ... 48-49
Letter to Fire Commissioner Johnson on incendiarism ... 49

T

Talbot, J. M., & Co., policy ... 34, 35
Tallman & Sears, policy ... 39
Teutonia Insurance Co. of New Orleans, policy ... 38
Teutonia Insurance Co. of Allegheny, Pa., policy ... 38
Tirnauer, Isadore, fire bug ... 79-83
Trade fires—Chapter IV ... 43
Percentages in various ... 44

U

Underwriters, Board of, New York—On "previous fires" ... 108
Report on ... 43
U. S. Underwriters, policy ... 39
United Firemen Insurance Co. of Philadelphia ... 39
Union of Buffalo Insurance Co., policy ... 38
Union Fire Insurance Co. of Paris, policy. 39

V

Vienna, fires per 100,000 of population ... 100
Virginia Fire & Marine Insurance Co., policy ... 39

W

Wade, Montgomery, Assistant Fire Marshal —In Steinkreutzer case ... 84-88
Policy in Liverpool & London & Globe Insurance Co. ... 31
Letter to, from Jillson ... 32
Wasserman, Hyman, self-confessed fire bug. 72-75
West 101st street apartment ... 75
Policies, lists ... 34-36
Westchester Fire Insurance Co ... 39
Western Insurance Co. of Pittsburg, policy. 39
Western Insurance Co. of Toronto, policy .. 42
Whilden & Hancock, policy ... 36, 39, 41
White, Major A., policy ... 35, 42
Whittle, J. H., policy ... 31, 35
Withers & Mills, policy ... 35
Williamsburg City Insurance Co., policy ... 31
Women fire bugs ... 90-99

Y

Yorkshire Fire Insurance Co., policy ... 39

Z

Zieme & Hallett, policy ... 35

www.ingramcontent.com/pod-product-compliance
Lightning Source LLC
LaVergne TN
LVHW010608110826
845149LV00003B/819